I0894129

Adventures in New Lands: Volume 6

Other titles in this series
Volume 1: *Journal in Greenland* by Hans Egede Saabye
Volume 2: *Inuit Folk-tales* by Knud Rasmussen
Volume 3: *Vikings of Today* by Wilfred Grenfell
Volume 4: *Tales of Yukaghir* by Waldemar Bogoras
Volume 5: *Eden of the North* by Signe Rink

The Diary of Johannes Hansen

Expedition to Eastern Greenland 1884-1885

Translated by Torben Hutchings
Afterword and footnotes by Signe Rink

International Polar Institute Press

Distributed by University Press of New England
upne.com

Originally published as
Vestgrønlænder Kateket Hansêraks Dagbog,
Copenhagen, 1900

Adventures in New Lands: Volume 6

Funded in part by a grant from
DANISH ARTS FOUNDATION
Copenhagen, Denmark

First English edition

copyright 2016 IPI Press
Design: IPI Press

ISBN 978-0-9829155-9-2

International Polar Institute Press
Post Office Box 212
Hanover, New Hampshire 03755 USA

Title page illustration: The East Greenlandic heathen drops dead from happiness at the overwhelming sight of seeing the Sun rise from the waves after another long winter.

Map of Danish Greenland

The Diary

I had heard, now and then, about trips being planned to Angmagsssalik on the east coast of Greenland, land of the heathens, but I never thought it possible that I might ever join such a trip, since I am a full time Catechist and am not at liberty to simply follow my own desires traipsing around the countryside. I ended up hearing more about it when I went up to the Juliannehaab colony where I joined my Pastor for a visit at the colony magistrate's house. When the topic came up, they pointed out that if I were to go I would have to pay for a replacement to do my work. So I gave up the idea entirely, since I would be putting my wife and children out in the cold if I left for such a trip.

By the time spring arrived in 1883, rumors had reached my own village in Agdluitsuppa *(see map, facing page)* that an expedition for

Juliannehaab had arrived and it would continue with kayaks on to Nanortalik *(Place of Bears)*, another Danish trading post south of here. They would spend the winter there in preparation for their expedition the following spring. They also planned to make small exploratory trips during the winter to eastern Greenland where they would cache food and supplies for the expedition.

The kayak men who brought this news also said that both my nephews, Johannes and Eric Petersen, would accompany the leader as interpreters, since they understood both Danish and Greenlandic–my sister Karen being married to a Danish craftsman in the colonial service at the colony. The mail carriers told me that the *Sâakutoq* (trip leader) also requested me as Captain next spring when the expedition started!

I stayed peacefully at home all winter, but when my pastor came through on his next south bound trip we went over the idea again. He said I could join them and that he would "take the blame," meaning: answering to the Missionary Council in Copenhagen.

⸸

So I left my home to set out southbound to Nanortalik on May 1st, 1884 after saying farewell to my dear Greenlandic pupils and my family. It would be hard to describe the heaviness of my heart, my wife's deep sadness . . . the children, who drifted away crying, then forgot their sorrow and came back to the same spot where we stood, unmoving, silently gazing into each other's eyes. We would not have been able to overcome such grief if there was no hope for my return. The trip was not bound for a place beyond our own borders, but the journey would be long and dangerous across the moving ice.

It was evening when I went down to the kayak that was bobbing in the fjord after a big storm from the North that was now easing out. My oldest son paddled with me for a while in his kayak. Along the way I met a few of those fellows who had accompanied the Minister on his recent trip to Nanortalik when he joined us to confirm several of the local Greenlanders, and who were now returning home with him.

I reached Nanortalik May 2nd to join the others in the expedition. I ended up waiting for a few days, since the *Sâakutoq* needed more time to find all the boatmen for our four kayaks.

⸸

The day before our departure from Nanortalik was a Sunday, so I held a service for our trips members as well as the Greenlanders in the village. I gave the lesson from Peter (2:11-20) which fit the occasion perfectly, since our expedition was bound for the primitive eastern coast, a land of heathens, seeing God seemed to be guiding our way that Sunday. We were reminded that God wanted us to behave as Christians when we met the heathens from eastern Greenland, as we soon would.

⸸

When we finally departed on May 5th our four boats were led by kayaks including my son Otto's. At Ikerasârssuk, the kayak men went ashore and fired their shotguns to send us off. Later we came upon Herrnhuts Mission Village at Narsak *(Valley)* where the German priests treated me ("the poor Greenlander") with the greatest of kindness.[1]

---

[1] *Since Hansen wrote these words, the Herrnhuts have left and the Danish Lutheran Church has taken over all missions in Greenland.*

⅄

On the 6th of May we continued, but when a *nigeq* (strong, eastern wind) began to blow we could not make any headway. Two more kayak men joined us at Pamiagdluk *(Long, Curling Peninsula)*, the southernmost trading post on the west coast, so now we had seven men altogether in our party.

We had to wait for some big icebergs to pass at Sangmissoq as they were bearing down on us; these became a familiar sight as we journeyed on.

The icebergs kept us waiting there for nine days; luckily the weather was fairly decent so our kayak men were able to hunt between the great walls of ice. I often went out shooting seabirds myself, and brought a couple home each time.

⅄

On Sunday I held a service in one of the tents. Ten days had passed since we had been surrounded by ice. We attempted to crawl along the shoreline by land towards the winter camp at Komiut *(Place of Earthworms)* but by the time we reached Qigssikátarfik *(Place of Earthquakes)* we had to pull up again, not very far from our previous camp where we saw the exact same heather and rock formations. One day I went for a hike in the hills to a viewpoint and upon returning I could tell everyone that I had seen open water at sea, and a ship. When our Europeans returned after a hike they had the same news, adding that the ship was a three masted steamer, *Pujortok*, which means smoke.

On the 22nd we made it over to Qumait where I saw a seal pup sunning himself on the surface of a very small bay. Just as I gave it a round of shot it began to sink. It was so shallow I thought I would be able to retrieve it. I did, which was lucky, since we were just starting to miss a true Greenlandic meal, as some of us were beginning to miss our home cooking.

Finally, for Ascension Day on the first of June, the wind died down and the weather improved. We reached the mouth of Ikerssaq which was choked with ice, forcing us to raise our tents at Akutdlinguaq. A north wind blew, which we thought might spread the ice out. We tried to slip in between the icebergs through Qipingajaq *(Water on Ice)* but the winter ice was frozen rock solid. We got through a narrow passage to Nunatsuk *(Secluded Place)* where we raised our tents on a site that was locked in with no open water visible in any direction. It wasn't a bad spot, to the North we could make out the Alik cliffs which looked very fine and delightful. When we went inland to the mountains we had a fine view of the sunrise. The sunrise on the east coast comes straight out of the ocean's horizon, and at sunset it sinks down behind the ice covered interior. At home on the west coast it is directly opposite. It was an amazing sight for eyes that had never seen the like before–a beautiful sight that quickened the deepest of thoughts.

On the tenth day after being surrounded by the ice pack we attempted to crawl along the edge of the land close to the wintering grounds known as Komiut. By the time we reached Qigssikaatarfik *(The Place of Avalanches)* we were stuck again and could go no further. We could still easily see the heather and boulders from our last camp, as the distance we had made was not very great.

On another day I hiked up to the hills and was able to report upon returning back to camp that I had seen open water and a ship. The other Europeans in our party who had been out scouting returned with the same news, adding that it was a three masted steamer or *Pujortok*.

By the 22nd we had reached the Place of the Earthworms, Komiut, where I got a seal pup sunning on the eaters surface in a small bay. Just as my shot gun fired he began to sink down. Luckily it was so shallow that I was able to retrieve it, and that was a good thing, since we were running out if good fresh meat and it would make a welcome addition to our rather limited food supply.

By Whitsun, June 1st, the wind had died down and the weather had improved greatly. We reached the mouth of Ikerassaq, which was jammed with ice, forcing us to pitch tents and set up camp. The north wind began to howl there at Akutdlinguaq *(The Place Between),* and we thought it might be the agent needed to separate the ice enough for passage. We tried to snake our way through the labyrinth of ice but soon found winter ice frozen solid and impassable. So we went around Nunatsuk and camped there, since there was no alternative. There was simply no open water as far as the eye could see. This wasn't such a terrible place, as its Greenlandic name suggested. To the north we could almost see the cliffs of Aluk, which were quite breathtaking. When we hiked up to the high point of the land the view of the sunset was unobstructed. Here on the east coast the sun rises straight up from the sea and it sets behind the ice covered interior, the opposite of our views on the west coast. It was spectacular for someone who had never seen such a sight, and quickened the deepest of thoughts, and even old legends. Once, long ago, a Greenlander from the east coast had been away from his homeland for a very long time and upon his return he rose from his tent after a night's sleep to see the sun rise. So moved was his heart from the beautiful sight of the sun rising up from the ocean waves that he fell dead to the ground. *(see illustration, title page)*[2]

We finally left camp at Nunatsuk, because of the ice and open water around Aluk Island, which takes its name from its shape, resembling a boot, had cleared. Of course Greenlanders always use /*i*/ where we use /*u*/ so they would call it Alik Island. The strait between the island and

2. *Illustration from "Eskimo Legends and Tales," H. Rink*

the mainland was known as Sikuijuitsoq, which indicates "Ice Pack that Never Melts," or the perpetually frozen polar ice cap. The mainland here was known as Sermiligssuaq.

We were laid up here for fifteen days of rain and high winds–sixteen people crammed into one tent. It became so damp that I retreated to sleep under one of the overturned kayaks. From the shore we shot at many seal pups, but they usually slid under the ice pack before we could get them.

Finally we made it to Kutsit *(Hip Bone)* and by the morning of June 29 we reached Qasingortoq *(Place of Echoes)* on the spot where the leader, Holm, had stashed a cache of supplies the previous fall. We discovered that the supplies were damp as the cave where locals had stored them had leaked, leaving them pretty much spoiled. The assumption was that they would keep as well as their own fat meats did, which were not aversely affected by damp conditions. Our guide had arranged for the East Greenlandic party to meet us here at this time this year. We fired off several rounds to let them know we had arrived and it wasn't long before five kayaks, including the bridegroom himself, who had promised to store the food supplies for us, arrived.

I had never laid eyes on people from eastern Greenland, and I found their speech and appearance fascinating and very different from our own. Towards late afternoon, some of the women arrived in the their kayaks. I was very surprised by what I saw, not knowing that I would be even more baffled by those who came later.

Navfalik, the bridegroom, was to be our guide, and we were supposed to stop by his tent for supplies. We were to help him unload but he had so many goods that some of the seal fat was left behind in his kayak.

When we left the camp we reached some small islands with yellowish heath or mossy turf, called Igutsat or "bumblebee" because of the black and yellow striped stones that looked like bumblebee markings. It was very difficult to paddle through the ice pack and the men with supply boats at first refused to even try. Finally we made it to Taateraat *(Seagull)* where we saw a few empty huts. On the following day we passed several large icebergs which I will talk about later, which we were quite worried about. The eastern Greenlanders called this place Quaralit or Angelicaland because of the abundance of the angelica flower. We could finally boast that we had eaten of the famous eastern archangelica root, but the stems were terrible! We met several more boats full of Greenlandic women. We passed many villages and tribal camps, and many families followed us north. I was preoccupied by the imminent dangers of the big icebergs and glaciers ahead, known as *puissortoq* because they shoot up out of the water suddenly and forcefully. Seal families also share this root name in common, *puiseq*. We were just a little south of them.

By July 4th we had reached Isortoq, known for its stormy weather systems due to river flows rushing down from the mountains, mixing with polar ice. We ran into impossible conditions forcing us inland at Inugsuk. Those boats following us also went ashore seeking shelter and we saw many abandoned shelters there. There was a beautiful waterfall and mountain side and many birds–auk, wild duck, gulls, ravens, terns and Arctic loons. I conducted a morning service attended by many heathens who listened attentively to my sermon.

The eastern Greenlanders gathered with us

told us about the story of a fish which had lent its name to that place in which it was not to be caught, mostly because there were plenty of other things to hunt, such as the plentiful shark which could be hunted with lines. Redfish and flounder could also be fished from the ice, even though it took plenty of line to catch them. Sometimes the biggest sealskins had to be cut up just to get enough line for those catches. They made fishing hooks from the tailbone of Harbor seal, strengthening them with steel tips when they could find bits of metal. During the high season for fishing they could load up their sleds so high that it was never necessary to take more than what they needed, since there would always be more in the future and no need to store the meat.

⁂

The following morning, July 7th, I climbed up to the high point of land to get a glimpse of the giant glacier which I had been feeling so intrepid about for so long, which I had named Puisortoq Glacier. It is so greatly feared that the natives never speak its name except in low whispers when they are in its shadow. Nor did they want us Europeans to invoke its true name, preferring us to use other more complimentary names, like "White Snow." I was not able to get a good view of it as it was covered in fog. I could see that the sea below was covered in calving ice mixing with sea ice. It would be impossible to enter into those waters with our boats.

July 9th dawned with terrible weather, rain and stormy winds, so we decided to cheer up by visiting one of the local ballad singers. The local "bard" was going to sing one of the sacred narratives accompanied by his sacred talking drum, which, according to the local custom, must not be touched by the uninitiated. It was highly entraining for us, as we had never experienced this kind of traditional tribal ballad or drum dance. The bard sat on the floor of the hut surrounded by a group of women who sang along as he began each verse. It sounded mysterious and was not hard on the ears. The drum was about the size of one of our biggest ash buckets from the hardware store on the west coast, about two fingers tall, and covered with the hide of a Ribbon seal *(Ugssuk).*

We returned the following evening to hear other singers from the mountains and chanters from other parts. Some of them played the drums and danced and women would also join in and harmonize.

⸸

On July 13th it was so stormy that I cancelled my service in fear that I wouldn't be able to finish due to the terrible roar it was making. I had written up the names of all the people on July 11th and counted a total of 82 in five women boats *(umiak)* paddled by seventeen kayak men.

Navfalik told us that in the North at Angmagssalik, where we planned on spending the winter, there were several murderers who had killed people just to eat their flesh. He said that on this side of the giant iceberg folks had stopped doing that long ago, and that the iceberg was the boundary between the two groups of people– the cannibals of Inugtumassut and the eastern Greenlanders.

⸸

July 14th. Today I tried to get two locals to tell me more about the lost tribe of European explorers that had come to Greenland, but nobody had much to say on that topic. At first they acted as if they did not understand what I was asking. Finally they told me a strange tale about a European and a Greenlander who got into an argument long ago. They tried to jump across a great chasm and the Greenlander luckily cleared the gap. The "Northman," as they called him, fell and was clinging to the edge of a cliff by his hands as his arms started to give out. His elbow broke and he fell down into the chasm to his death. On the shadow side of the glacier you could still see where he fell, where a pile of stones marked the avalanche that followed his fall. The narrator had not seen this himself, and nobody knew much more about "early Europeans" in Greenland.

They did tell me that in their region they had their own version of Spirit Land just as we had on the west coast, a place where the ancestors came from, now populated by strange or evil spirits who would one day come and possess them in order to destroy their culture.

Oqualurtaaq had a very different story to tell–that he had heard the noise of the glacier calving all the way down at their winter grounds, Anoritooq, a days journey from the glacier. The mighty, feared mountain of ice was also known for its ability to warn of pending deaths. There was a hiking party once that was preparing to ascend into the higher elevations but were forewarned by the sudden and strange appearance of thick and heavy fog. This was taken as a sign not to continue, and those who did not heed such warnings would suffer imminent danger and even death.

The people on this side of the land also told how they could catch salmon with the help of supernatural forces. They would hunt the salmon until it swam towards the foot of the glacier and then shoot it with birding arrows or spears.

Malkias, captain of one of the supply boats, announced today that he would not be following us any further, so we searched for his replacement among the locals. We found only one young woman was available: her name was Majivariaq, a nickname which meant "wandering Lizzie."

After some time had passed waiting there on the south side of the giant glacier, a woman asked me this question, "Where do children go after they die?" It was not easy for me to find an appropriate answer since the heathen population here does not share our way of thinking. My answer followed along these lines: When the body passes away, the soul lives on forever. The soul rises up to Heaven and meets God's son. When that happens the dead will be resurrected and the earth will dissolve and everything will fall away. But after explaining all this I asked them a question, "What do you believe is the story of the first people on the earth, and how did they get here?" The eastern Greenlanders all believed, they told me, that once two people fell down from Heaven and they gave rise to the people of the Earth, but how or why this happened nobody knew.

⁂

Oqalaurtaaq told me one day while we were waiting for better weather that there is a place on an island, Uvdlorsiutit, or Almanac Island, where salmon had changed to cod in an inland sea. He also knew about a place called Land of the Seagulls where fish had grown as big as walrus in an inland sea. The heathens up north were pretty much all able to communicate with the supernatural world, according to Oqaluartaaq, who apologetically informed me that he preferred to stick to the world views provided by the Europeans. Still, he went on, it would be hard to completely dismiss the powers behind their northern "Shaman" who could simply "will" a bear to appear and even get it to talk to a human. It never ceased to amaze him how the Shaman could bring around abundant seal during a time of scarcity and hunger. "Proof like that makes me a believer!" he would say, ending all further discussion.

⁂

We did not get any further, and we had so far to go! On July 19 we attempted to set off but had to turn back as the ice pressed us ashore. That day our west Greenlandic boatman Samuel capsized behind us and almost drowned before we were able to finally rescue him. He wanted to continue, and did his best to convince us he had fully recovered, but we insisted on going back ashore to rest.

I conducted the communion service the following afternoon with many local heathens attending. I showed Oqaluartaaq pictures from the west coast reader and explained the story of Jesus and the Creation story from the Old Testament. I also explained how and why the phases of the Sun and Moon change, as well as many other things, and he was full of wonderment at it all.

When the eastern Greenlanders heard about the big ships, they began to worry if these were the people coming to destroy them. These fears may have been rooted in legends passed down from earlier ages that saw the deadly arrival of the Vikings, whom they called "Northmen." I assured them that any ships that arrived in their waters would be carrying peaceful missionaries, supplies and trade goods. They should always feel safe greeting and meeting such new friends and needed not fear them at all.

I found a little deformed puppy that had been born without head or tale and was engaged in preserving it in a tin can to take with me. As I soldered it shut I had developed quite a curious audience for my efforts.

At camp I learned more about the invisible people in Greenlandic mythology. One spirit guide, called Ijaajaak, was able to return a lost soul to its living owner if it had been stolen by evil humans or witches.

⚲

By the 23rd we left camp again in fog and followed with three heathen boats. As soon as the fog lifted we went ashore again to get a good look at the giant glacier as we finally were ready to try and get around it. I went off by myself to pray to Our Heavenly Father and Earthly Lord for protection and safe passage. "You gave us all Creation, the dangerous and the placid, forgive us our sins, have mercy on us, help us pass this enormous mass of ice and we will praise your glory forever with our deepest gratitude! Hear my prayers! Amen!"

⚲

There is only one little island to be found along all of Puissortoq, called Ikermiuârssuk *(The Strange, Solitary Dweller)*.

The glacier's southern side is full of reefs, but deep waters can be found along the northern side. It is only during times when the glacier is about to shed ice, "calve," that it is dangerous, as the fallen ice blocks slam together with such force that they sometimes touch the sea bed, whereby they once more shoot upwards and are smashed to pieces through new collisions. This may be the cause for the belief that the sea has a bed of ice, which makes this place so feared. However, we did not see any sea bed of ice, even though the water was quite clear in most places, and, God be praised, we made it across the long stretch without danger; but the fog mostly prevented us in gaining a complete view of the great Puissortoq, leaving the impression of a "monstrous" ice field! As soon as we got under way, our east Greenlandic traveling companions shot away in their much lighter small boats without the slightest concern about what happened to us. We had, coincidentally, thought that they would have to turn around due to ice, but we were wrong about that. They had, by the way, let it be known that they would know how to "hex" their way onwards if things got tricky.

Once we'd overcome the glacier, we found them once more just north of it, where they lay waiting for us. We had to settle down here, as they were not prepared to proceed right away. Here our leader regaled each of the eighty two heathens with ships bread, with which they were quite delighted. Later I asked them if they had *kivisigpoq* (sacrificed) to the Puissortoq en route or uttered some magical spell? They answered "no," but this may have been because I had earlier said that such things were mere trickery.

Meanwhile, one of our own rowers asked me, just before we began the crossing, whether I was of the opinion that it would be proper to throw something into the water to placate the glacier; to which I firmly replied that she should simply stick to him, to whom she had given her promise in christening.

We carved "C_{IX}G.G.U.[3] 1884" into the cliff. And once we had rested at a very unsafe landing site, where I dared not leave the *umiak*, we proceeded onwards the next day in such a thick fog, that we once more lost sight of the heathens. With their smaller boats and much lighter cargo, they could always get through places while we, with our heavily laden boats, had to make one detour after another. We saw a number of promontories *(nunatât)* here and there poking out of the great land ice.

We then met up with our heathens once more, and together proceeded across to Tingmiarmiut, where the Easterlings had a wintering site near the "Seagull Cliff."

---

3. G.G.U. = Greenland's Geographic Survey.

It is said that the seagulls had left there when some egg collectors plummeted down from it.[4] Twenty three people lived at the wintering site at the time, but this number would increase by fifteen, as Navfaliks, our pilot's family, intended to winter here.

The stretch of land, which we had recently crossed, was nasty to look at, and frightfully cold because of the proximity of the great glaciers; whereas our current location is more like the regions of our own homeland, and this has immediately cheered us up a lot.

⁂

The only place where we had previously encountered a normal grave was all the way down at Alik and it was only now at Tingmiarmiut that we encountered another; as it is otherwise normal for the Easterlings to throw their dead into the sea. Those they don't do so with, they simply lay out on open ground, without any form of cover over them.

Up until now, if you ignored Majivariaq, the heathen girl, the expedition had only consisted of the original crew from back home on the west coast, but now the two Europeans–who were picked to winter at Nanortalik, the Danish

---

4. Understood as being due to the fear that the spirits of the fallen might reveal themselves to their unhatched young as avengers.

outpost from which the expedition had set out–were to leave us; and both their helmsman Gideon and kayaker, Lutevik, as well as the rowers, were surprisingly happy about this. And then I also, like our superiors and my nephews Johan and Henrik, wrote my last letter to my family–the last before I was next to see them again.

After the parting, we eleven that were chosen to winter at Angmagssalik proceeded with all our cargo split between just two *umiaks*, of which I steered one and the heathen Avâtlak steered the other. We had also obtained a new rower. Her name was Tamo. The day we took our final leave of our countrymen and the two Danish gentlemen we listed as the 30th of July.

On the 2nd of August we reached the little site of Tingijartivarfik *(Place Where Something Flies Out)*, where only three people resided at the time, and of which we found only one at home–namely their "old wife." She told us that her husband and daughter were out kayaking at the moment, as well as that the daughter had caught a small seal the previous day, but had also caught two large Bearded seals (*Ugssuit*) only a couple of days before. She preferred to wear men's clothes while at sea, the mother also explained, while she would wear women's clothes at home.

The former wintering site of a previous Danish traveller was pointed out to us further north, which was that of the Danish naval officer Graahs, from the beginning of this century, but who, on the whole, didn't make it nearly as far north as we had.

⁂

On the 3rd of August we found things to be somewhat ice free, at least as far as we could see from the lookout cliff, and we also succeeded in using sails as far as the Orquat *(Sheltered Side)* headland. Here the heathen Napârtoq left with his family to steer directly to Qeqertarssuaq *(Big Island)* which is usually their favorite summer site, while they mostly winter at Igdloluârssuk *(Dilapidated Dwelling)*.

We now gained a following wind once more, and, as we could now raise sails in *Sáakutôq's* boat, we were always able to remain somewhat ahead of the others–and we were thus the first to arrive at the strange place, Qimisâq, which is an island. A number of people from Sermilik were here in tents. Overall they included two tents and three *umiaks*.

As we approached, a great bustle started ashore. People ran around among each other and along the beach, and signaled to us where the best landing sites were for our *umiaks*. They generally turned out to be very friendly and gracious. Our eyes certainly widened with surprise though, as they were quite naked standing before us, reaching out with different things, such as skin scraps and leather straps. They seemed to know nothing of bashfulness.

When we finally put into the Fjord, they immediately made themselves useful in helping with the unloading, but they certainly threw our stuff around carelessly. Their womenfolk were no less gracious than the men, but while their attire was in no way as sufficient as that of our own women, it was in no way as bad as that of the men, who were only clad with a small belt, wherein all their amulets were sewn.

They were almost wild with happiness over our arrival, as they had never before seen Europeans, but of all the Easterlings that we had encountered so far, they were undeniably both the strangest and the most captivating. We did, however, encounter many like them later. They constantly invited us to eat, but always chose what we were to have, as such is customary with them. In the evening a couple of the men donned bearskin leg dressings.

Most of those who, on our arrival had handed us gifts, now gradually came back and asked for something in return for them.

While it was a Sunday, I did not hold a service,

as I was too tired to do so.

⚓

Wind and weather were against us the next day, but even if this hadn't been the case, we would not have been able to leave anyway, as our East Greenlandic traveling companions would in no way relinquish the great things that were offered them here, and these people were undeniably very generous. Some of the men of this place, who had been out hunting, only came home the day after our arrival. They found us to be very pleasant and appealing, they said. *Sáakutôq* asked me to write down their numbers and names.

One of them, whom they called Ajualik *(One Plagued by Boils)*, owned an *umiak* that was so small that the covering only required five skins. They drew forth a widow, whom they wished me to speak some comforting words to, as she had recently lost her son. He had travelled northwards hunting along with several others, but had not returned with them. I then explained to her what the Creator does with his Creations, not according to our will, but according to his– by soon making them happy, then soon sad once more; on how the Savior, who is the Creator's son, used to comfort the grieving and resurrect the dead. And she thanked me and said that we must be very happy, having such things to comfort us.

⁂

As we didn't move on the next day, I, of course, got the opportunity to speak to them about several different things, and I, among other things, questioned Anginâq *(Large Man)* about the Northerners, to which he answered that he had heard talk of them, but added that he neither knew anything about ruins or any other things they had left behind. Anginâq had two wives and a number of other housemates.

⁂

When we could finally leave, we also took leave of a few of the heathens, who had so far been accompanying us on our way, as they suddenly decided not to go onwards, but instead settled down at the various wintering sites which we gradually passed, and we only retained Ilinguanîs *(Dear Little Mate)* with us. Their boat was once horribly crushed in the ice. We were also soon assailed by a sharp southerly wind–which they called "*piterqaq.*" The guy-ropes parted almost as soon as we got them fastened, which was hard enough in itself, as we hardly had anything in this stoneless, icy land to weigh down the edges of the tents other than our own boxes and chests. While we lay over this time, I showed the heathens biblical pictures and explained their meaning insofar as it was possible. They were entertained and prepared to adopt Christianity, they said, but did not know how they would get round to the western coast to learn. This was of course just the same bad excuse which they used at every opportunity.

While we were still staying at Nuerniagartêq *(Place with Many Birds)*, a youth caught his first seal. This animal could not then, for ceremonial reasons, be flensed in the open air, but had to be brought inside the tent. Then the catcher's hair was cut, and the animal's claws were thrown in the sea.[5] From now on the youth was to be considered a man and provider for the family.

The next day, the 15th of August, the weather began to look ugly as we set off across the broad stretch of Pikiutdleq.[6] And as we lay here, poling our way forwards with axes and staves, the southwesterly winds started in earnest, but thankfully without quite becoming a storm; and

---

5. As an offering to Arnaquaqssâq – "the foul old woman" below the sea–who is keeper of sea animals.

6. Named after the tern or Sea swallow. The tern is an incredibly busy bird, with turmoil in all its movements.

thus we finally made it, unharmed but utterly soaked, to Putulik *(With Hole)*. Here Samuel and I alone ensured that the boats were safe, but no sooner had we finished our preparations for meeting the storm than it swooped down upon us. This daily duty was one of the worst of the journey.

The next day brought heavy snow clouds. I could not carry out our usual Sunday service, but instead tried to explain the meaning of Sundays to the heathens, which they seemed to understand somewhat, and were pleased to hear about.

The next day the weather improved somewhat. I was personally rather uncomfortable, with back pains, but could, however, help *Sáakutôq* (the leader) sew new ropes for the tent, as the last storm had torn off our old ones.

When we were ready to depart from here, our Europeans did not exactly have high expectations for good weather, in that their "*silasiut*"(barometer) wasn't looking too good and we soon had a very unpleasant *nigeq* over us. Our heathens' incredibly low *umiak* took in a significant amount of water; and before we got the tent properly erected the storm was upon us once more. To make matters worse, Severine–one of our best rowers–had now picked up a bad stitch in her side. To everyone's joy, however, kayaker Samuel caught a large seal, as we had by this point had to go without true Greenlandic fare for some time.

This was otherwise a horribly foul land–so completely iced over, that even the cliff tops (*Nunataq*), which are usually the only ice-free pieces of land to poke out of a glacier–were covered in hard, smooth ice. One should be able to understand how easy it might be for those who were already disheartened to start to have misgivings at this point with regards to reaching Angmagssalik, our approaching wintering site, where we wouldn't even be housed before we had to build ourselves shelter. It looked desperate, as even the sea began to freeze over between the floating ice-fields and floes. And how hopeless did our return journey back to the west coast look?!

The old man Ilinguangi who was an *Angákoq* (wise man and seer), told me about something that had happened to him last year. This was about the time when some of his site-mates had ventured out and been gone for a long time. He became sorely worried about their fate, he said, and when it again grew too late, he decided to use his secret arts, or "means" as he called it. First he wound strong seal skin bands around his head and laid himself flat on the *igdleq*,[7] with his face facing the rear wall of the house. Once there he immediately saw the wall open, and saw that which was invisible, namely, a couple of the missing standing, quite alive, shopping in the store at our previously mentioned West Greenlandic trading post, Pamiagdluk. But he was sorely saddened that he could not see his nearest kin, called Qitsikajêq *(Scratcher)* among them. So personally did he take it, he said, that he immediately had to redo his art. And, as expected, after he had once more strapped his bands tight around his temples–he spots Qitsikajêq–but at a place even further North than Pamiagdluk, namely Nanortalik. Here he saw the man standing, leaning up against a white wall, just like those of the Danish houses.

Finally, he had become calmed, he said. However, he had since had another vision of sorts relating to the return trip of the same people,

---

7. The continuous wide or deep bench, which, at a certain height from the floor, lines the entire rear wall of the Greenlandic house.

since, "by using his powers, he had seen them anew in the company of some strangers," he said, although he had not been "sufficiently powerful" to see who these people were. "But now I know," he added, "it was of course You!"– "Yes, what he says is all true," the other natives standing around us confirmed; and he had done many similar things before with the help of his "means!" (This is to be contrasted with evoking or foretelling with the help of summoned spirits). When doing this, he first took a piece of round cut dried Bearded seal skin, and kept repeatedly banging it with a drumstick, while he simultaneously drew the rustling skin back and forth (or in a circle) over his head.

This ended with the drum continuing to whiz around his ears and then he finally felt as if his head had opened, and he could immediately see his helping spirits. In this way, he achieved his intent, he explained; for he could now wish or demand whatever he wanted, for it would, from now on, all be fulfilled–such as, for example, discovering the reason why someone had fallen ill, or finding a way along impassable paths, and all such things! He had helping spirits among both the *Ingnerssuit* (The Fire-swallower Trolls) and the *Tarrajarssuit* (The Shadow Trolls), but he also had several among the "Great Spirits" who helped him merely by being summoned, and if only he now had his drum in hand, then he would have cleared a path through the ice for us.

Then he wanted it explained how it came to be that the merchants on the west coast sometimes used to buy skins from the catch of the fire trolls[8]–for his returning countrymen had not been able to explain it to him sufficiently. At that point, which (prior to us) was the furthest north ever to have been reached by Europeans (namely by Captain Graah), our leader plied his whole crew with coffee in his own tent as a way of thanking us for having been so obedient and successfully conveying him as far as this, and finished with the hope that we would soon reach Angmagssalik itself just as safely. For we could now see the blue mountain, which still, however, looked terribly distant! But it would have been nothing to speak of if the path had been normal water, but now–with our short day's journeys between the monstrous amounts of ice, and adding to that the night frost–had already begun to close every opening between the floating ice and glued the floes together!

When we finally reached "Graah's Beacon" we wrote the 25th of August. The next day we set off from here across the incredibly wide

8. People imagined the Ingnerssuit (the gnomes beyond the sea shore) as seal-catching kayakers, similar to Greenlanders themselves.

Ikerssuaq. And then, finally, one late evening, after a long day's slog in wind, rain and other difficulties, we finally reached Sujunikasik *(Land that Lies Ahead)* where our boat, that is to say, our leaders, was the first to reach land. We hurried as best we could to get the tent set up, so that the other boat crew could get comfortable as quickly as possible after they put in. But the rowers said nothing more in thanks than that "it was all the same" *(sussasoq)*, "for they might as well lay down and die here as any other place!" They were really discouraged and frustrated though. It cannot be denied that it had been a hard day for them as well as the rest of us! For here we now rested properly.

The next day, I once more spoke with Ilinguangi about various things: "Bear cubs," he said, "we prefer to catch with our hands. As newborn, they are generally as big as small dogs; the "old" ones they often take in their caves, which are easily the size as our sail-cloth tent (i.e. 10 feet); but these caves are otherwise completely empty; there is nothing in them at all other than the bears," he says. When I, for the fun of it, told him that bear cubs back home were no larger than a thumb, or no larger than that the mother carries them around in her ear–he looked surprised and said seriously, "No, it is certainly not like that over here!"

⸸

When we put in to Nûkajik *(The Nasty Headland)* the next day, we were met by an *umiak* from the Sermilik *(With Land Ice)* Fjord, where a large number of people lived, and as soon as the crew realized that they knew some of our East Greenlandic companions from down south, a scene of grief unfolded, as our people were informed that a shared relative had died back in the Fjord over the course of the winter. While one did feel some sympathy for them, it was hard not to laugh at the way they cried, and no sooner were they done than all was forgotten, then they both laughed and chatted as if completely indifferent, and they weren't overly concerned with their dead anymore![9]

They told us that many people had starved to death last year, at this place, which was called Inigssalik *(Dwelling Place)*, and that several had only avoided doing so by eating the flesh of corpses. The same was also to have happened at Qernertuârssuk *(The Strange Dark Place)*, where a widow had to consume her own family. Here

---

9. Hansen probably only wants to point out that the heathen scenes of grief were more ceremonial than a display of personal grief would be.

our kayaker Samuel had heard a woman mumble incantations or "*serrat*" over an *Ugssuk* skin, which she was in the process of treating.

The Easterlings tow their seals in a different way than us. A Bearded seal will be tied to the bow, but regular seals (*âtat*) would be towed at the stern.

At our next place, Ikágtoq *(The Shallow Inlet)*, we had quite a hard time understanding those speaking. But we were now so far towards our destination that the Angmagssalik Fjord opened up before our eyes, and with sails set, things proceeded quickly, so that we swept from Orssuluviaq *(Feldspar?)* straight across to the Tassiussârssuk *(Inland Lake)* headland. Here, in the little sound, I immediately noticed an old ruin of a house; but did I assign it any importance in that moment?–or think specifically that that would become our future winter house?! We went even further up the Fjord and finally encountered a couple of tents, which happened to belong to the residents of Tassiussârssuk. We set ashore here, but did not want to unload the boats right away, and as I was the one most responsible here, I stayed all night and slept as well as was possible on board. (One never knew what kind of people we had arrived among!)

The next morning I went ashore and wandered over to the house wall which I spoke of before and realized quickly that it could probably prove serviceable as the foundation for the house we now were about to make.

The heathens could not grow tired of looking at us. To begin with they had acted afraid of us, for which reason a large number of them had rowed away in their kayaks, though mainly to notify their local neighbors of our arrival. And it didn't take long before they came back in droves quickly becaming far too indiscreet and intrusive in that they had to touch and feel all our things. Sometimes they lined up quite far away from us and stared at us, and yelled "îh" and "âh"; and then someone said, "We are sorry for you poor things, for having come this long way up to our dismal land; but to us you are incredibly funny, and pleasing to look at!"

The next day we gradually started work on our house, but couldn't get anywhere because of the heathens, and it wasn't until the 12th of

September that we got things set up and now dared leave it as it was and go on a little journey around the area before the winter arrived in full. In order to get enough wood for the roof, we had to take one of our *umiaks* apart.

On the evening of the 14th of September I spoke with the heathens a bit about Creation and they listened very attentively. I asked some foreign kayakers, who had arrived to look at us, why they seemed so afraid of us and the reply was, "That it was because they thought we intended to eradicate them." I said: "How would we, who are so few compared to you, be able to do this? It would be more reasonable that we be a little afraid of you, as we had heard that you tend to kill each other up here." They responded: "îh! Why would we do anything to you, innocent as you are? It is only those that deserve it that we finish off!" "No," I said, "we wish you no harm. The reason that we have come here is simply that the Europeans, whom you see here, wish to explore your land to make the route around here easier, just as it is for your countrymen on the west coast, as well as educating you about Christianity!"

Shortly after this, an *umiak* arrived from Sermilik with the intention of having a drum-song with some of the people from here, but nothing came of that, as the others, the opposite party, or those they were to perform against, were not yet present, having not yet returned from their summer dwellings.

⚔

Sunday, the 7th of September, we held our first service since the landing. Several of the heathens were present, and were confused by it.

This same day was the birthday of the Danish Queen Louise, and on this occasion we were all plied with various things in the tent of our leader, Holm. In the wonderful quiet moonshine that there was that evening, we thought our future residence to be quite lovely and auspicious.

⚔

An old man told me that he once had his "soul" *(tarneq)* stolen, as someone else called Maratssuk had taken it and sent it inland, and he had not been able to catch seals while this lasted; but thankfully Augpalugtoq, an *Angákoq* from their site, had finally retrieved his soul in time for him not to die completely. But he now hated Maratssuk, as he generally had the unpleasant habit of robbing people of their "souls," and he had, by the way, killed his stepfather last year.

⚲

The next day, when we finished our entrance passage–which was also to serve as our kitchen–under roof, the basic elements for our house were now in place and we prepared to travel north in *umiaks* the following morning. We were accompanied on this journey by many heathens in kayaks. One of these, Alusakâq, told me that he had seen an *Avangiarssik*[10] last year, a small animal which was as big as a fox, with four legs and wings that it could use to fly, and quite a short tail; it had yellow and brown fur like a bear. To see this animal meant that a bear would soon be caught and that was also the case this time. It was he himself that had caught it.

⚲

An older man from Suvdluitseq *(Cunning Person)* told me, "We knew that you were going to come, although we had heard nothing about it." When I answered this by saying that he then must be an *Angákoq*, he first tried to deny it but later said "Yes," and that he had been notified of this in a vision which he had experienced inland, which consisted of him having seen a "monster" rising out of the cliff on the land opposite from

---

10. A mysterious creature which often announces itself through a strange whistling.

where he stood, with a torso as large as our tent and black and white spots. He had then immediately tightened straps around his head and laid himself down facing backwards on the bench and immediately felt like an *Angákoq* (able to predict events).

⁂

In a house at Nûrajik, where I counted and listed people's names, there were forty eight people. Those trinkets we gave to the heathens or paid them with, they traded away among each other, as they would otherwise do themselves a mischief with them, they said.

They throw the dead into the sea along with their possessions.

They blame us for the wind and rain which has lasted since our arrival here. They asked if we had noticed a large rock somewhere on their "land," which looked like a bear. This, they said, was what was angry with us and therefore worsened the weather, and when they spotted Samuel's gun, they suggested that he fire it at the cliff. They thought this would probably help.[11] In this house we also saw the woman, who, during the famine of the previous year was to have sustained her life, and that of her daughter

---

11. Greenlandic habit of pardoning oneself to European listeners, due to the cliff being in the shape of a Danish woman.

with the corpse-meat of eight people, whom they had gradually consumed. We were regaled with Angelicas here, but I had never thought to encounter such small and measly stems!

The shape of these people's kayaks is quite similar to those of us North Greenlanders with only the cross-straps (*tarkai*) being attached in a different way; for they are only placed behind the kayak hole and quite close to each other (with us, where they are distributed across the entire kayak deck). The stern is also higher than in ours. Their catching tools are not pretty, but the kayak oar is nice.

In speech they place a strong emphasis on the final syllable of the word and pronounce this in a higher tone.

They are hatefully inclined towards the residents of Sermiligaq, as they are supposedly evil "soul robbers," and they also warned us to be on our guard; and one evening as we prepared ourselves for departure, since the weather looked to be clearing, the heathen Ilisimârteq *(clever one)* came in to me and whispered the following in my ear: "When you arrive at Sermiligáq *(Large Glacier)* you should try to lure Maratssuk *(Obstructed Path)* over to you, and then shoot him;

for it is the very worst for "*Tarningêrneq*"[12]; he steals their souls so they become ill from the loss, and are sometimes close to dying." I answered as to say that Christians were not allowed to kill people, and that this wasn't what we had come here to do. I added, "I will even address he that you mention with love." Then he slyly sought to placate and beg something off of me, which I did not, however, let him have.

⁎

Another day, as we rowed between the many islands and land in the Sermiligâk Fjord in our *umiak*, we happened to spot a house remnant on the way, and then a Greenlander, in the process of pulling his catch onto land, and then yet another kayak, which came around the headland. Once the aforementioned kayaker spotted our boat with a raised flag, he suddenly stopped, and would not come closer until we had waved to him for a while. It then proved to be the aforementioned Maratssuk himself, along with his younger brother Sêrnaq *(Acidic Plant)*. "What are you called?" I asked Maratssuk, but he stated a completely different name, and the next time another one. But when I asked, "Are you not also called Maratssuk." He finally replied, "Yes, they

---

12. The collective soul of all things.

also tend to call me that." When we passed him our snuff tin to let him take a pinch, we noticed he had to hold onto our boat to do so, for his entire body was shaking.

He had said to Samuel later that he had heard the noise of spirits and that Tornârssuk *(a demon)* had stirred beneath the ocean, and that this had predicted our arrival. From here we set off directly across to the headland of Sermiligâq, as it was our leader's intent to climb the Fell from here. We then set our tent up on Uigordlerssât[13] at Núngarut.

⚔

We set off across the fell to Qissuit-kât the next morning; and after much scouting of all four corners, the expedition leader finally said, as he collapsed his telescope after having looked around with it for a while, "This shall be the limit of our journey, and the stretch of land that we have reached here we will call "King Christian IX's Land." And as he planted the flag, he continued, "This is the first time that this land has been walked on by Christians and Europeans. This island, which we have trekked inland on is to be called Erik the Red's Island, as he was the first European ever to come to Greenland." We then had our meal.

---

13. To attach or make part of.

Outside the sea stretched without limit to the North and South and was without ice. There were mighty waves at sea, but with not even the slightest breaking over any reefs. But furthest out, eastwards, we saw something that looked like fog over fells or mountains, and we figured that this was mist over Iceland. These were pretty and appealing sights, but it was cold, as the *nigek* blew, and suddenly it grew foggy around us, and the wonderful sight was covered, as were the mountain tops inland of us.

To mark the final point of the East Coast Expedition, we now built quite a high cairn, wherein we placed a document enclosed in a tin box, and the document contained the same words that our leader had stated earlier, to which was added all our names and some coins were placed on top of the paper (to weigh it down). "G. G. U. CIX 1884" was carved into the cliff itself.

Just as we returned from here, we encountered Maratssuk and Avgo coming to visit. They immediately followed me into my tent, and I sought to be friendly to Maratssuk, but I also asked him, "How did it come to be that people at Angmagssalik had something against him and the Sermiligâqs in general?"

"They have?" he answered, "though it was us

that had to flee in the Spring out of fear of them, and settle at Sermiligâq." After this I spoke to him for a long time about our Creator and Savior.

⚵

On the 21st we climbed a 2,000 foot high fell, which our leader Holm gave the name Leif's Island.

When I was invited to drink tea in the evening along with our Europeans in their tent, I was pleased by the good notice that I would be given a bonus on my wage of 300 kroner, and *Sáakutôq* furthermore thanked me for the help that I had been to him.

⚵

On the 22nd, the weather thankfully cleared. As our leader was highly reluctant to leave this spot (that is, the Sermiligâq Land) without describing the location of the different places in the most accurate way, namely with the help of the instruments that we had brought with us which showed "directions." But we eventually had enough of the place–for after we left it we soon had to return because of the ice, which filled all the waters around here. I then used this opportunity to go around to the heathens and write down their names. When I had spoken to them of the divine things, they said that they would come round and let themselves be baptized in two years time, but I still did not have much faith that they were serious.

⸸

When our leader had again studied the sun, we set off once more, but it grew dark before we reached Ikagtût. The Sermiligâq Fjord is difficult to travel due to its two ice-filled arms: one to the North and the other to the South. To enter it you have to set off at dawn. At Ikagtût *(The Very Shallow Waters)* we caught some wonderful salmon, and furthermore had an abundance of seal meat, both fresh and dry, that the residents supplied. The area around here is "pretty country," as both sides of this large sound are pretty, flat and climbable, and the hinterland is an equally pretty land, with high fells, as well as a large plateaux with an inland lake and a salmon river. But apart from this there were no traces that the "North-dwellers" had ever been there; only several tent walls could be found, left by the Greenlanders themselves, who tended to make summer journeys here. Even further inland, the area is pleasingly beautiful, but it is similarly certain that it has never been populated by Europeans.

When we left here on the 24th of September, hacking our way through the ice, the air grew heavy, but we made it to the Nûrajiks *(Strange Headland),* who had hauled down their summer tent that very day and moved into the winter house, even though they hadn't yet closed the window holes (with intestine skin. There is, after all, no way to obtain glass window panes here, or at any of the other sites, so they use either the aforementioned material or a slice of clear ice).

The house was big, with three building sections, and forty eight people lived there. ("House" always means the same as "living room." Thus, in this case, a three sectioned living room with forty eight people!) In the past one would have had a number of lamps burning, over which the large stone pots (which hung from ropes in the ceiling) would boil constantly. They were eager for us to stay, but this was not possible, as *Sáakutôq* was eager to see the base of the Angmagssalik Fjord. When we passed the fishing site here (i.e. the one the entire region travels to in the Spring to scoop up the little herring, which the Greenlanders call *angmagssaq*) we saw surprisingly large schools of wandering Fjord seals. It grew dark again before we managed to reach all the way in, so we didn't even bother setting up the tent, but instead slept on the ground. The country here is not that pretty. The fells rise almost directly upwards, in many places all but without lowland, but in other places where there was some, both flowers and bushes were to be found, but no crowberries.

⁎

At Ikagtût *(Where The Countryside Was Reasonably Fertile)* we also one day sent out the rowers to pick berries, but there were strangely not any here either. From here there is a crossing point to Sermiligâk, which the sleds probably use in the middle of winter. We went up the fell to see the view: 1,800 feet, *Sáakutôq* said it was. From there we could gain a better understanding of the base of the fjord, where the ice-fields are created–and it was jam packed in there. There was no bare land behind Sermiligâq's ice-field ejections–only ice-country–not as in the base of Angmagssalik which, as has been mentioned, is a beautiful fell countryside. At the fishing site, excellent boot straw (*pinek*) grew, of which we collected a bunch, as the ebb was simply so strong that we had to wait for the water to rise enough for us to set off, anyway.

When we came past Nôrajik again on the return trip, the wind dropped, so it wouldn't delay us to make a small visit ashore. An intense catch was currently beached here; seal corpses lay everywhere, both untouched and cut up–"*tagpinarmat!*" The sight could be considered overwhelming! They are otherwise impoverished people, and the rifle, they say, has chased away the sea creatures.[14]

At Qumarmiut, which was the penultimate place we looked past before we headed over to our own place–someone immediately told me that Qunîtse, their *Angákoq*, was to summon spirits, and that the lamps were to be kept doused, for there was to be a wife-swapping, as was customary across the coast, both each time there was a new occurance, as well as after certain celebrations.

There was a terrible heat from the many lamps and the many people were also all sitting around naked without the slightest embarrassment. They received us extremely kindly. The next day it snowed and there was a strong disturbance in the air. I spoke a lot to the heathens about our belief as well as about Christian traditions, and when I was done, they asked me to tell my people back home that they also wished to learn something and convert. I then asked them if they in that case would be

---

14. This Expedition was the first to Angmagssalik, so the effect of the rifle can not be considered a cause for scaring away seals.

good and obedient to their new teachers and help them if they were ever exposed to danger or distress. To this they answered, as if with one voice, "Yes." These people were of a milder and more gracious type than those further south.

Once when I went out to cool down a bit, an old woman came hobbling out after me in the entrance passage to gift me with two seal flippers as well as some crowberries (of the kind that they prepare with a mixture of blubber and store in the stomach of a seal as winter supplies) and said, "This is as thanks for telling us something we have not heard talk of before; so if you like it, eat it." When I told her that nothing was needed in return, she said, "Yes–this is the custom among us when we celebrate and something new comes to us *(nagliutaringata)* and you caused something like that today, as this is the first time we have heard of that which you told us about."

Finally, at the last place where we put ashore, namely at Ingmikêrteq *(Place Off By Itself)*, which happened to be prosperous at the moment–we were told that there was a hot spring on the other side of our dwelling. *Sáakutôq* immediately wanted to see it while we still had a boat in the water. Many kajaks followed us on our way, but when we caught strong winds out of Ikerasaq so the seas beat against us, most of them turned around. A few still wanted to come along and see *Unartok* (the "warmth"). However, we had to turn back this time, without having found the spring. The "warmth" was probably quite insignificant, seeing as the spring could hide itself so easily. There was a freezing cold easterly wind, to explain why I was freezing quite horribly when we set out from the Sarfarssuaq *(Place With Big Currents)* isthmus the next morning.

I have yet to tell you about something strange which came over me just as we were about to steer into our future home. It happened when I saw the Greenlanders that were here, the children in particular, run along the beach to follow our boat. I suddenly felt like I was home on the west coast–and that the children were my own, for they also came running to meet me, just like that, when I returned from my trips. The world spun around me until I finally found relief in weeping; but I had to bottle it up as I was being impertinent to the others. It pained me all day. It was practically a form of "ecstasy" that I had been experiencing.

We finally reached our wintering site, where we were now ready to completely settle down, and this took place the last day of September.

Angmagssalik

(The place with herring)

1st October. Early in the morning boats arrived from other sites to offer dried seal meat, as well as seal stomachs with blubber to sell or trade. People from Qumarmiut were particularly determined to stay overnight with our neighbors[15] to dance. I was ill and could not go with the others to view the spectacle, but instead laid myself to rest. I had slept soundly when they returned home. We still had to sleep in tents, but I managed to install windows in the house the next day, and at that point we Greenlanders preferred to move inside, in spite of the fact that no panels had been placed in front of the walls. The next evening I was able to attend the festivities of "our neighbors" myself, while they were planning to "sing against one another" again. This time it was Maratssuk and Pîlakât *(Lghtfingered).* They charged around as if utterly mad while they sang, drum in hand, and hurled accusations at each other,

---

15. The designation "our neighbors" will, as a rule, always refer to the natives sharing the mainland with the Expedition.

charging and butting one another as animals are wont to do.

It now began to get very cold, so even our Europeans preferred to move into our, as of yet incomplete, winter house. The next day our umiak might almost have blown away were it not for the fact that we had ensured it was sufficiently weighed down against wind and weather. Thankfully it was not damaged. A blubber bag of one of our neighbors was ripped away into the sea and lay drifting in the strait below us.

Later I carried out a service for the first time in our winter house. During my subsequent visit to the heathens, I explained to them the importance of Sunday to us Christians, as I had previously done to the people who lived further south. They were otherwise up to other shenanigans; the men played at straps which they had to try and pull away from each other. Both straps and other items which the winner was then to keep. The women sat working with various things and sang while doing so; some of them sewed, and others scraped skins. The heat was terrible, in spite of the fact that there were just two pots over the lamps. Once the food cooking was finished, they all ate.

The next day kayaks arrived from Sermiligâq and they notified us that Akajînaq's *(The Sweet Little One)* son, Sauniko *(Gnawed Bone)* had suddenly disappeared from the site. He had only gone outside to catch a couple of seagulls that had settled down by the beach, but when people later went out to see where he had gone, he was nowhere to be found and they were utterly convinced that *ingnerssuit* (beach-gnomes or the so-called "fire swallowers") had grabbed him. Their *Angákoq* had subsequently confirmed this by inquiring with other gnomes through magic.

On the 9th of October we intended to go to Kangârssuk *(The Strange Big Sea Promontory)*, but instead had to creep round to the *umiaks* due to heavy seas; and this proved useful for us, as there lay an abandoned house (which was allowed to remain in peace from the heathens, as they were afraid of it, due to it probably being haunted) and from this we collected no small amount of fuel. The house had been abandoned during the famine winter five years ago, where only three people had survived. The bodies had partly been left lying within the house, and some skeletons, both whole and broken, lay spread out over the space outside the windows. It was not, however, believed that anybody had been forced to resort to eating corpse meat.

The journey here was to be our penultimate one before the winter, and we now settled down completely–but of course we had daily dealings with our mainland neighbors, and in a way also with the other sites–but now it was always them that came to us.

Today *Sáakutôq* has calculated that our house site lies with Tassiussârssuk on the 65°37' North latitude.

⅄

On the 21st of October we created a scaffold for our *umiak.* We were later visited by our mainland neighbors' oldest–Qutsuluk *(He With Broken Collar Bone)* was his name–and when he saw the wood which we had brought back from Umîvik *(Beaching Place for Umiaks)*, he took a piece of it to make an amulet for his son, as he could tell that this driftwood had previously belonged to his own grandfather.[16]

When a group of men, recently headed home after a visit to Sermilik returned, they reported having lost Pîlakât in the heavy seas. He eventually turned up, later on, and people were

---

16. The spiritual worship of the old peoples include the belief in the protective influence of grandparents over their grandchildren.

convinced that he had had the protection of *Ingnerssuit*.[17] He too was of the same opinion.

The resident *Angákoq*, Sanimuínaq *(He Who Walks Sideways)* has been off evoking spirits at the Kangârssuks, and he had several kayaks from there accompany him home. There he hexed Amatsinek *(One Willing to Carry Children on His Back)*, whose finger had swollen up after having recently cut up a (presumably rotten) seal that had been stored away. Through this investigation it emerged that the "soul" of the index finger had been stolen and carried away into the hinterland. For this information, the patient paid him a puppy in return.

I asked Sanimuínaq how he went about establishing that the "soul" was gone and in what way he had returned it? But he would not answer.

On the 26th of October Sanimuínaq listened in on our service for the first time and was gripped by it; "Won over," he said.

The next day brought an offshore wind

---

17. Ingnerssuit are not visible to the kayakers they take care of at sea, at least not from a distance.

which had lessened somewhat over land. Our leader and my nephew Johan had been on a visit to the heathens and seen how they went about flensing a Harp seal. When they had opened it, the men scooped up the blood with their hands and drank it. They then cut the meat into pieces and gave it to their women.

The men were naked, apart from around the loin, where they wore their short leg garments.

The heathens share the catch with each other. The person who caught the seal just gets the head and one flipper for himself, or, if there are a particularly large number of outsiders present, the head alone. When a bundle of dried meat is brought forth, the wife of the owner splits it into as many pieces as there are people in the house, whereafter the man goes round and gives each of the men their share; but the children he feeds each by name, and only then does he keep that which remains. In this way the Easterlings share everything between themselves, and nobody views anything as completely their own.

Kayaks from Umîvik came here offering to trade small items they had made: birds that could nod their head and pick up feed, "spinners" that could turn with the wind, and other Greenlandic toys.

It can easily be understood from this that the Greenlanders were not necessarily taught this by Europeans, but must have known these crafts even before their appearance. One story, which we read to them from our West Greenlandic textbook, they seemed to know; but another that we read, they did not. I now asked them to tell me one of their stories in return, and they then told me one called "The Old Bachelor With the Iron Cheeks," but this was just the same as the one we told at home called "The Greedy Atdlarneq."[18] To be fair, he did tell it in a slightly different way to how we did. Our leader later wrote down many of their legends.

While the Umîvikers were still with us, Pîsâq from Qumarmiut came here to ask whether we knew what had happened to his brother, who had said the day before yesterday that he would row over to visit us. We notified him that he had been here, but had left again the same day. Pîsâq headed back to his kayak immediately after that, crying. It subsequently turned out that the brother had not died, but had simply rowed over to visit Kangârssuk. As we ourselves also thought that the man must have perished, we questioned the Umîvikers on what customs followed a kayak foundering, and they answered: for example, nobody from the site would go out in a kayak

18. Atdlarneq = A piece of clear sky among the clouds when it starts to clear up following bad weather.

for three days, but would sit at home to mourn over the departed; though those that were not his nearest, could continue to go out catching, if they wanted to. Both outsider *Angákut,* as well as locals, tended to head out to obtain information about the missing person, and it was furthermore customary not to observe song parties for five days following the death (*iverssorneqarnaviangilaq*)

At the exact same time, we had to wait in vain for our own Samuel. We sat up waiting for most of the night, and during the later part of the next morning our women began "The Crying"[19] for him, while I myself sat and regretted making my journey here. How was I to manage without him, my good assistant in everything? But thank God, he did return! He had simply to make the decision to go ashore yesterday, rather than potentially getting himself even more lost in the whirling snow than he had already been. He had no idea of where he was at the time of his decision, or that he had been as close to home as it later occurred that he had been.

19. In using this expression, Hansen reveals that "the crying" over a deceased, as in West Greenland, is in part ceremonial.

⁎

The same evening I escorted two of our women and *Sáakutôq* himself on a visit to "our neighbors," to see Sanimuínâq carry out *Angákoq* tricks, and evoke spirits. The youngest men of the house set everything out for him. They whetted the drum and placed it on a flat stone to the left of where he was to sit on the floor, and in front of the door opening they hung up a couple of water skins[20] and, similarly also, one in front of the nearest window, as well as one to sit on. Then he took his place. He was naked with the exception of some small straps (around the waist and over the shoulders–these were his amulet bands). He sat down with his face pointed straight at the door, and his feet touching the door drapery (the stiff water skin). Then he bound his head tightly with a very broad strap. When they were ready to tie his arms behind him, they wanted me to do it, but I refused. Then they moved his arms round to his back themselves and tied them together with a quite long strap, in that they, among other things, put the loop around his wrists, but they didn't let the arms come together completely. This was done in quite an artificial way, so it made me think that

---

20. Water skin is unhaired. After treating, the skin is very stiff; it was this skin which was used for producing the noise that was to accompany the drum of the Angâkoq during his spiritual incantations.

the *Angákoq* probably knew how to release himself when the living room grew dark.

The next thing to happen was that he began to shake all over and hiss as if he were terribly afraid, and then they extinguished all the lamps, starting furthest away in the southern end of the lounge. The flares were reduced gradually until it finally grew pitch black. Then he shrieked: "*ijâh - jâh*," initially like someone afraid of something, and then with sounds that are impossible to describe or imitate. It was certainly not a song. But Johan, who has been to Europe, compared it to the sound that the railway engine produces when it starts to roll away. Now the sound of the drum became quite strange in its vigor; and it really sounded to my ears as if it were spinning freely in the air above his head (that is to say, as if he was not beating it himself with the drumstick or with his knuckles as it would be when it was used openly at dancing parties or when they "sang against each other").

The audience could be heard yelling "*Kâ-hû*" ("come on"), from one corner at one moment, another corner the next, to lure the spirit into showing itself, while the skin which was hung over the door made an indescribable noise. (Maybe so that the *Angákoq*, who presumably now had loosened his restraints, could better "treat" them). He let his own voice be heard along with this, whereafter unknown voices were heard, both from above, and from below–beneath the floor; but the covering skin crackled even worse than before. Now the unknown voice had come so close that we heard it shout "*amô-amô?*" and this ("*amôrtoq*") was the chief of *Angákoq*'s helping spirits or *târtoq*. His real name was actually Qimmaraq *(The One You Flee From).*

He now also began to leap around the living room, both across the floor and on the benches, where he touched and felt everything–and people too–so they screamed and were frightened. Then he finally reached me and felt me from top to bottom. Then someone shouted "*amô*" again to egg him on or tease him, whereupon this *târtoq* went wild. The voice sounded foreign, but I could not mistake it for anyone else's than that of Sanimuínaq (who must therefore have been an excellent ventriloquist). When he had felt me, he also allowed me to run my hands up and down his body to convince me that the one I touched could not be the same as the one I had previously seen tied up (thus someone else than the *Angákoq* himself, whom I was to believe firmly tied up in his restraints).

After that he once more began to sing–nicer songs than the usual ditties–and when he was done with this the skins once more began to crackle terribly while one could, through that, occasionally distinguish the barking of a fox. This voice then began to speak, and asked, as its owner simultaneously sniffed at us, "Who could we be?" To which some of the audience answered: "Yes, you are right, it is quite right that strangers have come here from the South!" And on requesting our names, some of these were mentioned to the one that barked like a fox. But *Angákoq* did not use normal words in his speech,[21] for which reason I could not understand everything he said, even though I sat closest to him. Now he asked me my name, but to this I only answered: "I am one who has come here to take steps for all *Angákoq*, and all spirit-evoking to cease around here, as I have no faith in any of it."

Then he said something again, to which I again answered, "I don't understand what you say and this must be because I am a Christian Catechist; but to this he replied: ("*Pyt*") "No, the true reason is that you walk around worrying about your wife and your children back home."[22] Then he let me feel him again and began to sing. It was as if the voice progressively became more and more like *Angákoq*'s original voice again, in that the previous one (Amo's) seemed both to vanish through the floor and ceiling, while all the

---

21. Angákut have their own language which is primarily based on a routine distortion, partly of the pronunciation of a word, and partly of its meaning, but also in more pictorial interpretations.

22. What is meant here is that the person in question was, under the pressure of his sadness, not to be considered sufficiently level-headed to have an opinion on "great things."

other noises–both those from the coverings and those from the drum–sounded the same.

Then his own voice spoke to the people, and when *Angákoq*, slightly after, asked me to feel him, he was still tied up; and, as his voice lowered, or seemingly exhaled, all the lamps of the house were relit once more; and then several people in the house exclaimed, "How can one not have faith in someone who can do such things?" But to this I answered that I would first like to think some more on *Angákoq* being bound! But they said that it was as it "should be." Then *Angákoq* himself shouted, "Now hurry and let us see who will be the first to walk outside!" Whereupon the boys and the young people all rushed off with *Angákoq* in pursuit, as soon as he had, of course, dressed himself.

When he came back in again, I told him I must, however, wonder over how you astound your followers so! He protested a bit over this. But when the rest of us came to agreement, we expressed our mutual admiration for *Angákoq*'s great skill, in that we could simply not conceive that it was purely he alone that had portrayed both of his "spirits." For the fact that it was a matter of learned arts, and not a revelation/apparition was something we were all convinced of. The fact that the audience was of another opinion and believed fully in the appearance of the spirits we had to view simply as being based on the ignorance of these poor people. I had, for safety's sake, brought a box of matches with me from home, just in case something terrible were to happen, but I had no use for them.

⸸

They had previously, when they came to invite us, asked if I would conduct my service for them, but to this I answered in the words of the Apostle: "'What fellowship does justice have with injustice, and what fellowship does light have with darkness.' No, I will not conduct a service for you!" Of *Angákoq*'s helping spirit, or the one that said "*amô*," they explained that it was a little man with a pointy head, who lived in a crumbling stone; whereas the one that barked like a fox was a creature that resided in a dried out lake.

Old Qutsuluk once told that he had heard mankind descended from two people, who, after the first Earth was destroyed, and the new Earth had come into being, had fallen straight down from the sky.[23]

Similarly, he said that the East Greenlanders knew that there had once been a great flood

---

23. This creation legend did not originate in Greenland. Indians and others have similar legends about people and animals that have fallen from the sky.

on Earth and had wiped out all humans and animals.[24]

On the 3rd of November we were visited by quite a number of kayakers from Qumarmiut. One of these described the spirit-flight of the *Angákut* in the following way: They bound him in the usual way, and bent him over by tightening the bindings from the neck down around the knees. He can not get up himself, as this is very painful for him, and his drum must, on this occasion, be able to move by itself; it then dances over and lifts him up, first by the head, so that he sits upright, and then by lifting him in the same way by his backside. Finally he gets on his feet, and then he, who is about to fly through the air, walks around on the floor for a time, whereafter he lifts himself up and floats around a bit inside the house until he finally seats himself on the drying rack beneath the ceiling, and then finally rushes straight through the roof or the wall, out into the air. Meanwhile the drum continues to dance of its own accord while the tied *Angákoq* flies around in the long, cold night, and gets as far away as is necessary. In all this time his

---

24. All other Eskimos have legends of a great flood which once destroyed the Earth. The Aleuts called it "aljack", which is one of their words for "sea" and "wave".

housemates sit in the dark, expecting his return, which sometimes happens at dawn. Even then, his drum still moves. But when he returns, he will either have been far away on the Earth or in the Heavens, on the Sun or the Moon. But, they added, these days there was no longer anybody who could carry out an air journey; you had to have seen someone else do it in order to be able to do it yourself.

⁂

Severine, who was one of our rowers, has begun to pay too many visits to the resident heathens, and once, I think on the 6th of November, she didn't come back at all. I told her what my opinion on this was; but she excused herself, barely, with the weather, and when I repeated my opinion to her a second time she was insulted and ran straight back there once more.

⁂

Pîlakât was the first heathen who ever asked me to tell him something about the first people, and about God and our faith. I of course did all that I could. I similarly carried out "explanations" for the others over in the "houses," on the following Sunday, with accompanying pictures, which I allowed them to ask questions about; and it ended, in the usual way, with them saying that they envied us, who had such good things to believe in, as well as that they would like to convert, but couldn't get round to the west coast for lack of rowers.

On the 20th of November, we were visited by kayaks who came to sell bear meat and skin to our Europeans. *Angákoq* Imaluqutsuk was to have evoked spirits over at our neighbors, but his drum had simply not wanted to be lifted, he said, for which reason he had finally had to give up. His helping spirit was otherwise supposed to be an *Ârrûssaq*–a spirit that belongs to the "white spirits," and thus the best kind.

As for the chief spirit or *Tôrnârssuk*, the greatest of all helping spirits, he said that he could no longer be able to view this as a good helping spirit, since the Christians round on the west coast called it "evil." Besides, he said, the East Greenlanders' *Angákut* also used it for evil and deceitful purposes, i.e. to help when they wanted to rob a human of his soul.

Qutsuluk similarly explains that people here at Angmagssalik calculated the time of the year in such a way that they marked the Moon they saw for the first time after the shortest day.

One day we were suddenly visited by all the men from our neighbors, and the occasion was that Pîlakâts wife was to give birth to her baby; and they mentioned on the same occasion, that anyone who lived in a house with a woman giving birth had to move all their clothes out of the house for as long as the birth endured. In good weather this was easy enough, but in bad weather they had to stash it away under the *umiak* (which is lifted up on its supports over the winter with its bottom facing skywards, thus creating a sort of roof). One also donned new clothes where possible on this occasion.

Among our guests, also, was the places *Angákoq*, Sanimuínâk, and since my nephew Johan once previously had got him to call forth his "helping spirit" so that it sounded as if he was really speaking out of the panelling, he asked him to repeat the feat again now, and I joined in this request, as well as promising that I would pay him something for it. But, he answered, "My helping spirits are not at my service on this occasion, as I have sent one down to Peqitigssak *(Land with Ammunition)* at Ingmikêrteq since he is sick with boils and needs help; and the other is with the woman giving birth. Thus I cannot get them to speak here." Sanimuínak's chief helping spirit is also *Ârrûssaq*; he was to have obtained it after a female *Angákoq*. Of this "spirit" it was said that the corners of its mouth were always red because of the amount of soul-blood it had been plied with by its first owner, specifically the female *Angákoq*.

The next morning we learned that Pîlakât's wife had birthed a daughter.

⸸

On the 24th of November Samuel caught a Harbor seal.

⸸

On the evening of the 30th, almost all of us went down to the heathens, where I wanted to perform a service, which they had requested of me several times now. First I asked them to sit down and be quiet, and then to listen well. I used the Gospel: "The time is fulfilled, and the Kingdom of God is at hand, convert Yourself and believe" (Mark 1:15). They listened well, and were glad of what they heard, they said, even though they hadn't really understood it. And a little while later they asked if we wanted to see some of their customs. I answered that I had nothing against that, provided there was nothing inappropriate about them. Then they began to dance in a way which was not repulsive. It was the first time we saw the women dance. They danced forwards in rows of three, one after the other, with drums in their hands. The first was a married woman, the second a little girl, the third an aging married wife, in *nâtit*.[25] As soon as the dancer began her song along with the rhythm of the drum, everyone in the house sang along, and as the song grew more joyful, the movements of the dance also increased as they twisted their bodies through all positions and to all sides *(tivfaserneq)*. The men also danced, but always facing the entrance passage or the house door. The men danced in a bent position, as if squatting, and beat three beats at a time on the drum. But learning their songs is very difficult.

On the 1st of December we were visited by *Angákoq* Autdlâgdlak, whom I had heard performed his art in a peculiar way–specifically by rubbing his drum against the floor. I asked him why he did this, and he answered that he in this way reached the point where he at least could cure illnesses in himself as well as in others. Through the rubbing, he made his "spirit" speak and provide advice. His helping spirit was a "bristle worm," and he usually repeated its words

25. *Nâtit are the quite short skin trousers which were probably originally designed only for indoor use.*

to his housemates, so they received its message at the same time he received it from the "Spirit." *Angákut* are generally not able to cure themselves.

This morning Alussagkât had snatched some pearls for himself from the lounge of our Europeans, for which reason he was not given permission to come in when he returned on the evening of the same day. I myself had been invited to join them for the evening meal. I must truly feel sorry for our superiors, who are often plagued by having their lounge filled with these Easterlings, who both disturb them in their important works and fill the lounge with the bad smell of their dirty leather garments; and then don't even keep still, but constantly run in and out of both our rooms: our own and our superiors.

Tikajaq explained that their *serrat* (magical incantations) lost their power when they were misused, for which reason he never used his carelessly, and to utter them without payment he would never do; for without this they would lose their effect all too quickly.

⸸

Their way of calculating the approach of the Solstice is by paying heed to the star *Agssîts'*[26] height in the sky; and now, on the 6th of December, people indeed came from Umîvik with the glad news that these stars had just now been seen to rise. One could now look forward to the Sun soon coming to a stop, after its slow descent, and thereafter begin to rise anew so the days would grow longer.

⸸

This evening I got truly angry with our womenfolk (*arnartavut*), who are quite irresponsible, and furthermore touchy about it, and easily offended. They never want to listen to my sensible advice and predictions, and, when I wanted to reprimand them this evening for their bad behavior, they deliberately made a noise with the harmonica to avoid listening to me. In the end I fled outside in my kindled rage. However, after a short stay in the open, it settled, so that I could go in again in a more mellowed state of mind.

---

26. Agssît here seems to be the name of a specific star or group of stars. Agssît can otherwise be found in several of the Eskimo tribes outside Greenland as a description of stars in general.

⁂

Over by our heathen neighbors, where I conducted a service explaining the Ten Commandments a couple of days later, this time attempting to use their own dialect wherever possible. They subsequently told me a great deal about their customs and faith:

The first Earth, they explained, was smooth and flat, and had neither mountains nor sea. But since "he up there" didn't like the humans who lived on it back then, he destroyed it, by which the humans fell down into the open cracks in the Earth and became fire-swallower trolls. After that, the Earth came into being, once more, but this time completely covered with glaciers; and when this once again began to disappear, two humans fell from Heaven, populating the Earth.

Yes, that was how they had always heard it told by their ancestors, and so they now told their children in turn, they said. But, they added, they now notice that the land ice (*sermeq*) which was now there, receded and grew less each year.

⁂

Narsingagtag *(Snub Nosed)* explained that as he once wandered back and forth outside on the house site, he had suddenly spotted two *Ingnerssuit*. They were dressed in leather clothes, just like the "real people," and had very small noses–almost no nose at all.

The Sun is a woman, they say, and is called Sungula; and the Moon is a man and he is called Ijâkâk, and the two of them were siblings when they lived here on Earth.

On the subject of shark fishing at Umîvik they explained that there were so many animals that one man might get twenty in one night. The meat and the liver they treated by first simply heating it without adding water, as it gave out so many juices itself; only when this juice had been pressed out would they add freshwater and cook the meat properly.

Narssingagtaq and the other storytellers had, by the way, come over because social festivities, "*katigssutainait kímiaqangitsut,*" were to take place over at our neighbors, and our people also wanted to go and watch.

It was Uvâjarneq and Mitârneq. Agdlagdlaq *(The Favorite)* had been dressed up as a woman with a blackened face, and then bound with criss-crossing leather belts, and he had a peg in his mouth which distended it out to all sides.

Thus he ran around and chased everyone, both around the floor and up along the benches, so people everywhere fled in fear of him. After him came Angitingivaq, also dressed as a woman, both with pearls and various other things. He similarly danced with a drum in his hand, but his manner was meek and simply pleasant to watch.

⸸

Narsingagtaq had also been there on the 16th of December, as our people were visiting our neighbors. He evoked Spirits for them, and was told by them that our Expedition had been accompanied by a "soul"[27] on the way here. Utuaq said of Agdlagdlaq that he actually should have been *Angákoq*, and had been a certain amount of time away from becoming so, but had suddenly become ill in his feet. The most important reason that he hadn't managed to become a complete *Angákoq* was, however, that he had not been able to keep his intentions quiet. He did continue practice obtaining "the shadow trolls" or *Tarrajarssuit* to be his helping Spirits though. These live in the hinterland and have human form, but are much smaller than us. He was not entirely unskilled as a Spirit-evoker, in that he supposedly succeeded once in getting

---

27. These souls would split, or veer slightly to one side so the others, not being visible, simply walked straight through them–it is said.

a faint glance at them (i.e. winding himself up to such a level of ecstasy that he believed he could spy them through the gloom). This had achieved so much that he once had been able to cure his own feet, which he had contracted an illness in. He had evoked these Spirits with the use of *serrat* or incantations (his private prayers, one must think).

"*Serrat*" are almost similar to prayers, but one can never figure out who they are being directed at. Thus they also utter them when it thunders, as well during solar and lunar eclipses. Utuaq added that when it thundered, they used to take a piece of *kukarnât* (dried seal blood) between their teeth so that this would keep the mouth properly shut, as those who were not careful to do so would be grabbed by "the thunder" (the Spirit of the Thunder) and dragged upwards with it, but then be dropped, whereby one, in the fall, would risk breaking one's lower jaw. People often stash away some *kukarnât* from one thunderstorm to the next, but it is a long time now since it thundered last.

When *Ilisîtssut*[28] were to make *tupilak* (a tool of vengeance in the shape of a doll, which they

---

28. Those who use magic to kill or torment or for other evil purposes.

purportedly later bring to life) they always see about obtaining a piece of clothing or something else which has belonged to the one they wish to harm. *Angákut* can sometimes prevent the intent of the evil hexes, but often they don't dare!

On the 18th of December, I went further up in the fell than before, whereupon I found out that the sea was full of ice, but strangely enough a strong swell was noticeable inland. The air was clear and I finally saw, with my own eyes, the Sun rise from the sea, but only for a single second, and then straight back down again!

Our Europeans had supposedly been told by our neighbors how the *Angákut* got their drums to spin around by themselves, but they had promised not to pass this on, so that it would not be rumored among the other Easterlings that some of them had been telling tales.

In the old days, the Easterlings fetched a strange rock from Qûjûtilik north of Sermiligâq, from which they made pearls. The pieces which they broke off looked like frozen *tugdlerungnat*,[29] and made for particularly pretty head and temple jewelry.

⸸

Today, Sunday the 21st of December, we had to keep the lamp burning throughout our service. I sought to cheer up my companions as best I could, as they now, so close to Christmas, were quite downcast by thoughts of their relatives back home. The next day I created a little Christmas tree for our Europeans by tying twigs and heather, which I had hidden away for that purpose, under the snow around a wooden stand which I myself had shaped into the likeness of a tree. Otherwise I would not have had the wish to do anything during these days, but would simply have been tormented by the thought of my children, who must now miss me.

⸸

24th December. Sleep eluded me last night. Over the course of the day we were visited by Utuak *(He Who Prefers Cooked Food to Raw)* and his son Qaoqortôq *(With Wide Forehead)*. I told them of the big party we're to have today, but it was doubtful that they were paying attention,

---

29. An herb which looks like a leek, the root of which has an astringent but pleasant taste and is eaten wherever it is found.

as they were noticeably captivated by some bundles of dried meat which we had brought out for the occasion. Things were quite scarce for the poor people at this time! As soon as they had finally headed off again, our women set to work sweeping our little living room, adorned themselves with new clothes and put up their hair. And gradually our depression and longings were replaced by satisfaction and well-being; and we all gladly listened to the words of God.

We were later all invited to eat with the Europeans in the living room next to us. Within it their Christmas tree, fashioned from twigs from the ground of Angmagssalik and decked with various things, and with candles on it! I quite forgot that I was in a place where no European had set foot before! Our own Europeans were happy and pleased. We sang lovely Christmas hymns and went around the tree, and later on we ate rice pudding and drank coffee afterwards.

My mental state did not quite reach that which I was used to at home at Christmas, as I was not with my children. But in a way I had never before truly celebrated Christmas as I did this year! And the entire Christmas period was like this! The first day of Christmas with our happy, uplifting service, and the second with a party with our superiors, where we played cards for small items, danced and had a meal. I only took part in their dancing out of sympathy for them, as there were so few men!

On the first day of Christmas the wind was terrible, with one thing or the other flying skywards, or at least, almost. There were not many heathen visits in those days. The one most eager to visit and take part in our service was Utuak's son Qaoqortôq. But due to superstition it is impossible to make him take his hood off of his head while he resides with us. I had criticized him for this ever since we arrived, and during the service itself I tucked it down around his ears without further ado. There was also a time where he resisted eating seal lung; but we finally (the poor wretch must have been too hungry) managed to convince him that it would be okay, but there is nothing to be done about the hood.

Nâqortôq's *(He With the Big Stomach)* wife at Kangârssuk had in recent days gone mad and accused herself of being a "hex." She had had a stillborn son, for which misfortune her husband blamed her, as he believed that she had not taken due care.[30] He split from her without further ado and sent her to Norssît *(Furthest from Headland).*

⸸

On the last day of the year we had the most wonderful weather, with no cold at all, for which reason we spent most of the day outside the house. A number of heathens buzzed like flies around us. I tried to speak to them a little about the meaning, for us, of the end of the year, but I did not succeed, as they had been blessed with no calm from these conditions at all.

⸸

This, the last day of the year, we spent most comfortably with *Qavdlunârtavut* (our white Europeans) who were *Sáakutôq* (the leader of the expedition: Holm) and Knutsen, who of course was a Norwegian, and whom the Greenlanders called Quaralik *(With Flower Tuft).* We awaited the midnight hour there and were given both coffee and punch and small gifts during the card game. And when the clock struck twelve, Holm congratulated us and thanked God that the old

---

30. Had the stillborn child been a daughter he would probably not have been overly affected; but the wife had to be punished for the loss of a son—as she had robbed him of his eventual assistant.

year had ended so happily for us all, and similarly hoped that everyone might be with family and friends in good health when next we meet! And we each hoped the same, of course. As for our superiors, I would like to say this: that they, right from the time we started living with them in the Spring, had dealt with us all with a true brotherly kindness, and they had similarly shown the heathens a lot of kindness and thus laid their Christianity bare.

Today we heard that an *umiak* with six healthy young seal catchers had left here several years ago with the intent to remain away for three years total, but since they failed to return after that time had passed, it was thought that they had either perished on the way or starved to death while there.

It was also said that another man once, a long time ago, had also been up north, and that he had encountered a tent site where he found both stored seal and walrus meat as well as a large walrus tooth! Other than this, these were the only times it had been noticed that people lived north of Angmagssalik.

1885

We who had overwintered celebrated the first day of the new year with joy, even if we were a little dispirited over our separation from our loved ones. However we all firmly hoped to be reunited! The next night, a "switch off" (wife-swap) was held over at the heathen site due to the scandalous custom they practice when male visitors come to the site. Two little boys who visited us the next day spoke plainly on the matter. The poor things were of course not raised to see anything strange in any of that which we Christians consider improper or immodest.

Our rower Cecilie had, during one of these days, almost frozen to death carrying water for us. Samuel caught a hungry Arctic fox, which was calmly eating from our blubber bags with his hands, and Knutsen shot it.

Sáakutôq is now measuring the height and width of each Greenlander who comes to visit us.

I must repeat that I have more than once been displeased by the behavior of our rowers during our stay here, as they often set a bad example for the heathens. But my reprimands are wasted on them.

A strange custom of the Easterlings is that each time they have bartered something from us–for example: a knife, a metal arrowhead or something similar–they considered it necessary to barter it away immediately among themselves–that is to say provided they had given us leather in exchange for their own catch.[31] We later heard from Utuaq that he had lost his *Angákoq* ability by once having recast some tin into a ring around his bird dart (we might thus imply: which he had obtained through European channels?). His *Tôrnaq* (helping Spirit) was to have been a jellyfish the size of a large Hooded seal.

It was from *Angákut* that they had gained knowledge of life in Heaven, they said. It consisted of lowlands, with quite flat hills, tremendously overgrown with crowberries, and in the sea of Heaven lived no other fish than

31. *Trade goods must be neutralised before they can be used by heathens, or, using the Eskimo turn of phrase, "must first be robbed of its tôrnârssuqtaq," its demons.*

whales,[32] and such things comprised the only food people had there. During their air-journeys, *Angákut* regularly visited the Moon, but the Sun was too hot to reach. The Moon was akin to a strongly burning lamp, the glare of which they could dampen by holding a water skin between themselves and it.[33]

On the 15th of January I was out hunting a bit, but as usual I saw nothing to shoot at. There was a southerly wind with only a two degree chill. As I dropped by to see the heathens on the way home, I found them to be very quiet and disheartened. For they were now starving. However they soon asked me to tell them something, which I immediately did; although of course not anything on matters of faith–as they were, bar one, "nothing but women." The only

---

32. This monotony of diet should be understood as a compliment both to the Sea of Heaven and the immortal "residents." Mátak (whale skin) is the Greenlanders' most favored food.

33. "The water skin" plays a role in the Moon Man's story–and as a Greenlander, he still goes hunting each time he visits the Earth. In the legends it often happens that the Moon's assistant (sometimes brother) Nelarssik (The Vega Star), is often clad in water skin clothes, while the Moon himself is clad in bear skins when the two appear together. In the East Greenlandic Moon legends, the two of them often appear as friends, but for the most part they are enemies.

man currently at home I found standing with his face directed towards the exit, evoking spirits with the help of his drum, while rubbing it.[34] What he learned, in this way, was, among other things, that his son Pilakât was not at Ingmikêrteq as he had thought, but at Nôrajik. It was also on this occasion that he received the important information that it had been his own wife, who the previous year had hurt the entire site by eating seal spleen (at a time when this food must be forbidden her according to the conditions–*agdlerissaraluaminik,* in abstinance). While he rubbed the drum against the floor, he constantly mumbled to himself, and then one or more of the women shouted, "Get up–get yourself upwards–someone has arrived who wants to see this." He kept rubbing and shouting, and then the others shouted back, "Uvánga," ("We're here") and then another voice– "Yes, it is like that–that is the way it is," and more of the same.

I myself understood nothing of this, but when I asked for an explanation they always simply answered "that it happens to be that way, and such is the way it should be!" How terrible and meaningless everything is which these poor people believe in and do! And how little one might begrudge them being given access to the one true God! But we must await God's hour!

---

34. Belief can "move mountains" after all–we say: "make tables dance" etc. The Eskimo simply replaces table with "drum."

For as Jesus said: None can come to me unless the Father that sent me draws him (John 6:44).

⁂

16th January. Today Sanimuínaq came over in a sled, but since he only had three dogs harnessed in front of it, progress had been slow in the deep snow. Regarding the treatment of the dead, we were today told the following: As soon as breathing begins to decrease, the dying person is brought out of the house, where they are laid out exactly as they are, without being sown into leather as in West Greenland; and if it is a kayaker, then they just pull the hood over his head, and then bring him to the "Shingle of the Fjord," from which they let the next high tide carry him out. This all happens with the grief and lamentation of those present. But on the occasions where solid ice lies along the shore, they have to knock a hole in it into which to lower the deceased.

⁂

18th of January. Today we discovered that bread had been stolen from one of the provision sacks which we had cached out beneath the overturned *umiak*.

My foster daughter Cecilie and our kayaker Samuel now view themselves as married, and believe that the blessing of the Church can be given afterwards, once we have returned home once more. This has caused me some sorrow, however.

26th January. Quiet weather with sunshine and only a 12° chill. Samuel and I had worked on shoveling snow away from our provision chamber–for it has drifted badly several days in a row.

I heard mention of a new custom for the first time today: When the Easterlings are unlucky enough to lose their hunting bladder in the middle of the seal hunt, they know that they will also lose the seal; this is caused by some creatures, who call themselves *Mákakât*, who steal both from them. They run down from the high headland they live on, and snatch the creature in the same moment the seal hunter sets his mouth to the water to call his friends for aid (*êrtarângat*).[35]

With regards to the "souls" of a person, Narssingagtaq explained that there were many of them–seven, he added. The largest lived in the larynx and in the person's left kidney. These were small people the size of a *qúpangnâq* (snow bunting), while all the others were only as big as a finger joint. Should an *Angàkoq* (we should assume a deceitful *Angàkoq*, otherwise he would be the healer) one of these small souls, or "*Tarngit,*" then the body part in question will sicken; and only when the true *Angàkoq* puts this "soul" back in, will the human fully recover. But if this does not succeed, then he must die. But when the "soul" of an actual *Angàkoq* is stolen, then it would become an evil spirit or a dangerous ghost, which was called *Qardlimaetseq*.[36]

I asked how it could be that a soul that had been eaten could "walk again"? But since he could not provide an answer to this, I tried to explain to him the Christians' thoughts on the soul, which has no body, and which will live forever as a spirit, and await the blessed resurrection of its first body.

---

35. Êrtarneq is the method by which all kayakers call for help while at sea, by placing their mouth to the surface of the water and shouting "éh". The sound is said to reach quite far.

36. Qardlimaetseq (written elsewhere as "qardlimaertaq"). The direct translation of the word is unlikely to be adequate and is therefore omitted.

Today, Sunday the 25th of January, there were, for the first time, no natives present during our sermon. Knutsen got a White fox. Later in the evening we were visited by a couple of Greenlanders who were probably hoping for some food. There was supposedly also a great lack of food at Umivik, and it became more and more common for them to try and pilfer from us, for which reason we chased away some of those who, during this time, came with the excuse of having something to sell. At Sermilik, inside the fjord, they were completely enveloped by ice, and three men who came walking over the ice said that they suffered great distress there.

On the 1st of February we experienced the most wonderful weather, and now we all had the desire to get out a little bit with a gun over our shoulders and hunt. I went with Ryper to Sarfakasík *(Place with Rough Current).* We met three Sermiliaks on our way. One had been in the water beneath the ice. This was terrible, as there was a 24° chill, even with the quiet weather. I shot four seals, sadly without it being possible to get a hold of one of them.

⁂

When we came out of the house the next morning, we found that all the ice had vanished from the Angmagssalik Bay, which scared me, as three of our rowers, Debora, Haldora and Severine, had left across it to visit Kangârssuk *(Cape Exposed to Breakers)*, and might now have drifted away with it. As usual I gave them sufficient warning–but what did they care!

⁂

We write now on the 7th, and the shark hunt is thankfully in full swing in several places around here!

⁂

It is reported that Sanimuínaq, who went to visit Kangârssuk yesterday, today brought back a new wife. But his real wife didn't like that at all, and she grew so angry that it ended in a fight, ending with the husband throwing his knife at his old wife. A couple of our people, who happened to be visiting there at the time, were so frightened by this that they ran away home and reported it.

It is to have enough children to help with the work that the heathens take several wives, or when the first only gives birth to girls. But Sanimuínaq had already had two sons with his!

When I was visiting our heathens one evening I saw a new custom. Utuaq had caught a seal, and as soon as he brought it inside, he dipped his fingers in the urine tub and smeared it over the head of the seal, before the flensing began.

On the 9th Johan and I went out to fish from the ice. I reached the bottom with five lines attached to one another. We were originally looking for redfish, but we caught none. The wind was offshore, and in the afternoon we went over the ice on a visit to Umîvik. On the way we met many Greenlanders from the various neighboring sites, who were also wandering round to visit each other–both men and women, and many with their Infants in the leather bag (*amaut*) on their back.

On the 13th, since the weather was similarly nice and mild, I once more felt the urge to go for a visit and this time went to Kangârssuk with the intention of staying there overnight. On the way I met a sled with six dogs harnessed and loaded with an immensely big Fjord seal. Space was nevertheless made for me, and things flew along.

At Kangârssuk I only disembarked for a moment, but promised to return once I had peeked back round to the people at Norssît. They were very glad that I would return. Here too the *ítoq* (patriarch) of the house returned with a good Fjord seal.

And when I returned from Norssît, where there had been a good catch, we sat up late into the night and I spoke with them on matters of faith, and as usual they praised how happy we Christians must be. I almost didn't sleep at all, as they had not given me anything to cover myself with. They switched off all the lamps–perhaps in my honor?

The next morning the wind had risen to a storm, and they asked whether I had the means to quiet it? The men, however, all went out hunting, while I remained sitting for a while to speak to the women. They told me, among other things, that this area had once been quite populated, and that people never suffered any deprivation at all. But then a terrible famine winter occurred where people died in droves, and they thought that this might have been a punishment to them "in their foolishness," not having sufficiently valued their fellow people, and had started to become mankillers (*silaqangipatdlaleramik inoqatinguatik toqútarmatigik*).

When I finally had to go, an old woman, who had a pain above her lower back, asked me to scratch her a bit on the outside of her furs with the bone of a bear, and when I laughingly did, I was gifted the bone.[37] Upon departure they also supplied me with both fresh and dried meat and an old man was kind enough to follow me a good part of the way home–"for he was worried about my fate"–he said.[38] That was Tikajak.

During my absence Samuel had caught a very large Bearded seal. He had now caught forty in total.

---

37. A similar funny event happened later at Angmagssalik, where a man who suffered from a boil asked one of our Europeans whom he encountered writing, whether or not he would "write a bit with the pen on the painful place–for then it will probably recover."

38. Hansen has, in a couple of places here, mentioned that some animosity was harbored towards him–specifically by the older man, whom he had reprimanded at the start of the winter, because of the suggestion to lure the killer Maratssuk out in order to shoot him.

19th February. Today we had a number of guests from round about and I felt a great urge to speak to the heathens right from the start, but I had to abstain from this, as our womenfolk were also particularly determined to speak–although only about very insignificant and meaningless things, so that the Easterlings, had I kept speaking, might easily have been given the idea that God's name was to be classed along with the "inconsequential." I did not want them to think that, so I preferred to remain silent.

Paussuaq *(Brawler)* from Nôrajik had been on a visit to Sermilik, he said, and that they were no longer completely without food.

Samuel fell through the ice today as he tried to haul in his shot seal. Luckily I managed to help him, and asked him to run home as fast as possible and leave me to take care of the seal. That day we wrote 22nd February. It was said that Avgo had gone over the ice to Ingmikêrteq with two of his wives, when it became necessary to leave one of them lying behind, as she could not keep up any more due to frost bite. But the other two had reached Qumarmiut, when Pîsâq *(The Very Poor One)* had immediately headed out to bring the almost dead casualty home, in spite of the fact that he was poor and only had a single dog pulling his sled.

A man called Qiainaq *(Weepy)* said that he fully believed in *Angákut* and as soon as he thought he was missing one of his "Souls" he would make haste to relay this to one of them– and then he gets them back, right away. But how the insertion actually takes place, he doesn't personally understand. He only knows that it tends to happen at night, or when the house is in darkness; then the *Angákoq* lets him sit down while he sets everything in order around him.

The wife that our *Angákoq* Sanimuínâq once brought home with him has now gone back to her own previous settlement. It is rumored that it was because his other wives had found her neither "pretty nor pleasant" (suffice it to say: found her superfluous).

Some small boys from our neighbors entertained us in a most funny way today, with competitive singing as they charged one another like mad animals, while hurling accusations and everything else that follows. They were incredibly funny and sweet to watch.

A large "Singing Party" of a similar kind was held recently at Nôrajik, with the exception that it was deadly serious. It was between Qunitse and Akernilik *(Hollow in a Glacier)*. From what is told, Akernilik raised an accusation against Qunitse's mother-in-law: that she, the year before last, had been guilty of eating corpse meat. Maratssuk, who had been present at the Singing Party, and who told us this, said that Qunítse's wife had been really angry (on her mother's behalf) but that the mother herself had been indifferent and simply twisted her nose and stuck her tongue out at the accusers.

Utuaq's wife gave birth to a son.

I spoke with Avgo, who visited us here on the 8th of March, for a long time about his belief and that of the Christians. For he is an *Angákoq* and has a dwarf auk as a helping Spirit.

Of Qîalineq, to the north (the place the previously mentioned hunters never returned from), he said that there was supposed to be plenty of both bears and narwhals, as well as that the Sun never sets there, but always remains at the edge of the water (as it goes round from west to east).

His father, he says, was called Maya *(nickname for spoiled children),* and he had once been round to trade in the shop on the west coast.

Today–good weather–not a cloud or any

breeze, and a chill of only 10 degrees. We had a bit of thin ice on the water here, while there was no small amount of heavy seas further out, as the pack ice had for the moment drawn away from the coast.

Angutínguaq told, during his visit, how he once, while young, had fought with a she-bear. When the bear had come at him to attack, he had stood quite still in front of it and had struck it in the face with his bare fists, but then the bear tore a gash in his chin, from which the scars were still visible. It also tore both his upper- and under-fur completely to bits.

"And back then I had such good strength that I could easily lift quite large boulders as if they were nothing," he said.[39] "For a while the bear had no power over me. It first threw me to the ground so I lay on my back, and when I finally, with great difficulty, managed to turn myself around, it planted its teeth into my behind. But I finally managed, with great effort, to get back on my legs, and then pierced it in a single location with my "*tôq*" (long pole with a bone– or metal–point), so it died on the spot. As I had brought my sled along, with good, healthy dogs before it, I quite quickly made it home, but in a terribly swollen state, and had to remain at home for a long time."

---

39. This sport previously comprised a specific branch of the Eskimo youth's upbringing. It is often seen illustrated in drawings.

Another oddity about Angitíngivaq was that he had climbed the Napariak *(The Vertical)* Fell at the bottom of the Angmagssalik Fjord, from which height one had a view of both the sea and of lands which one cannot see from below.

Our rower Haldora is not well at the moment. The weather is also bad and the swell comes in heavily from the East; and we don't see many heathens outside for the time being.

On the 12th of March I once more lived the high life and ate both lunch and dinner with my superiors–this time on the occasion of my nephew Johan's birthday. Two Greenlanders who had not been by here for a long time gave us various bits of information about the customs among their countrymen, and dwelled in particular on the mutual love the heathens share, especially in times of want, where they tend to share everything amongst each other, he said.

On the 13th of March we were once more worried about Samuel's absence in the kayak, but once more it went as before: with him coming home in one piece with a large seal–and there was much joy, as we had had to go without true

Greenlandic food for a long time.

⸸

16th of March. In the expectation that the expected solar eclipse would be complete, I went over to our neighbors, whom I thought, maybe, would display some particular customs on such an occasion. But in this I was disappointed–the solar eclipse was also only partial. However, they did say that Maratssuk's father–(the aforementioned Maya)–had once spoken to the Sun during an eclipse.[40] Otherwise they didn't have much to say. The didn't fear lunar eclipses either, they said. The Sun was eclipsed up until the half-way point, but since it was cloudy, it was not easy to distinguish overall. Some of them revealed their fear as they asked me, "How would things end if it went completely dark?" They greatly admired the Europeans, who could predict when such things would occur.

⸸

The 17th of March. We heard from the heathens that Sanimuínâq had evoked Spirits because his son had become ill.

---

40. "Spoken to" means that he directed a prayer incantation (serraq) against eclipses to the mighty celestial object itself to avert the danger threatened to the world.

It was similarly said that someone had now seen two Snow buntings. These couldn't be migratory birds already this year, but rather a wintering pair. Atdliartortôq *(The One Who Grows Quickly)*, who came from Nôrajik, gifted me a piece of *Mátak* from the whitefish they caught there earlier in the winter. They suffer no deprivation there.

The 20th of March. The weather was nice, with a mild wind and a chill of only 4°. On the same day, just as we all sat around with our things, our women informed us, yelling as loud as they could, that there was a seal splashing about in the water just outside our windows. Johan and I were not slow and ran straight down to the fjord–I, with Knutsen's breach-loading gun, which I loaded on the run. I had grabbed a couple of cartridges as well, but as I was ready to clean the end of a thread away from the cock, the shot went off. That is to say, I just heard a bang and thought it was Johan who had fired, but then, after a prick in my finger and a jerk of the gun, I quickly understood that it was mine, and that I was injured. One of my index fingers hung by a small bit of skin and was pitch black. I ran straight up to *Sáakutoq*, who sat at the table drawing maps. I showed him the finger, which I felt it would be best to cut away entirely while the hand was still numb, and then I cut it off myself with a pair of scissors, whereafter Holm removed the broken bits of bone and bandaged it. Unfortunately I could no longer be pleased by our wonderful seal which Samuel had now had to catch alone, as our leader forbade me seal meat for the sake of the finger. The heathens themselves otherwise tend to eat a portion of it when they are injured, in order to make the wound heal up as fast as possible.

I will, by the way, bring my good old index finger back to the west coast, and I have for that reason placed it in spirits.

Sanimuináq's mistress, who had left him because his other wives hadn't found her "appealing," had later come to belong to Mitsuarnianga *(Dipping in Water)*, but had now finally been called back by her first husband Nâqortôq (the husband who previously divorced her over the stillborn child).

27th of March. Clear, quiet weather this morning, chill of 17°. Absolutely no open water. The pack ice has set in heavily. Samuel got two Fjord seals. Pîlakat came in and thought that he had heard a sound, as if one of us had called him. We didn't really believe him; he probably just came to see whether there might be some seal meat to be had! He certainly stayed here until late that night. My finger is very carefully checked daily by *Sáakutôq*, and I was sorry that he would have to deal with something quite so unpleasant.

⚓

On the 1st of April, which was Maundy Thursday, I did not perform a service because of my condition. It was terribly windy.

⚓

On the 3rd, Autlâgdlâq came to stay with our neighbors; and the day after that Ukutsiaq's *(Region of The Heart)* wife died. She had had terrible internal pains.

Ulingneq's *(High Tide)* husband has perished in a kayak. He had capsized just in front of his own house, but since the ice edge was too high, and people thus couldn't come to his aid quickly, his death was unaviodable. The wife–that Avgo once had to leave behind, half dead, on the ice at Ingmikêrteq–is still very grief stricken, and will probably never recover.

Qunîtse's wife gave birth to a daughter in such a storm that it was almost impossible to have one's effects brought out of the house, as per custom.

Sanimunínâq's wife had healed Uikiaq's other wife, who had been ill for some time. For this she had been given a bow drill in payment, as well as sinew thread and some leather scraps. We heard, among other things, that Sanimuínâq (the *Angákoq* of the local heathens) had once, in a storm that he'd been having trouble getting through, had sent out one of his guardian spirits, who supposedly immediately quieted the storm, which was a hard northerly. Agdlagdlaq believed fully and firmly as usual in the veracity of this.

Today, Good Friday, our leader was not pleased with my finger, but since he did not prohibit the performance of a service, I explained our "Gospel" as well as I could for those present. This time there was, of the Easterlings, only a small child present.

In this time we often have difficulties with the many Easterlings who come sniffing around after food, and we are often almost unable to obtain enough for ourselves, since we don't have more to rely on in these lean times than our daily rations of Danish food, and as soon as the heathens know that we have something over the fire, they don't budge from the spot. One can of course sympathize with them, but in spite of their poverty and deprivation, they don't make the effort to go hunting, and they are generally nowhere near as brave as our West Greenlandic kayakers.

I have been given much reason to love our Europeans since I lost my finger! This is primarily because of the great kindness they show in taking care of it!

⚓

Today I heard news: Naqitsilik said of his sister–the one who still lay ill after her bad ice journey during the winter–that she had shunned her own daughter with Avgo, over which the daughter, out of sorrow and shame, had thrown herself into the sea. For that reason Naqitsilik would no longer overly care if her "despicable" sister were to die. She was herself a widow, and did not for the most part live particularly honorably either. She had most recently left Sámerssaq *(With Strong Posture)*, since the latter's real wife was always offended and angry with her. How lamentable it is to hear these poor people sit and say such things for all to hear, as completely as if there is no sin or shame involved. They don't even think it is wrong to let their children hear. In a way they can be somewhat pardoned for this, as they all live in a single room and have nowhere to send the children away, even if they wanted to. However it is simultaneously also their wish to raise their children with knowledge of their customs by letting them be present for everything. They only demand that they obey their parents and the adults, and avoid doing what they forbid them, such as, for example, touching the drum or trying to do magic.

The heathens have the scandalous custom that they, at the new Moon, travel around to wife-swap. This has always been the custom, as it had been with their ancestors they say, and they view it as permissible. But if a man on the other hand keeps an additional wife in secret from his real wife, then the latter will be terribly "*ningartoq*" (jealous).

⸸

5th of April–Easter morning. As I was unable to sleep, I got up very early. The sky was cloudy and it wasn't particularly cold. It was pretty, and I felt in good spirit! True, the state of nature here was not like that of our own homeland's heralding of the Spring, with the heat of the Sun and the encouraging bird calls, but here was at least the hope that one might soon expect to see the gulls return. This the heathens had told me.

Yes–Easter had come without us yet having seen so much as a fly stir, but the grace of God had not for a moment left me in doubt of the joy of the resurrection–and I celebrated with thanks to him–a wonderful Easter morning!

Our Samuel contributed greatly to our temporal well-being as he, over the course of the day, caught two large Bearded seals.

The 6th. Today Avâq *(Back of The Head)* came. He came from our mainland neighbors, where he was to examine *Angákoq* Sanimuínaq, through drum rubbing. For the latter said, with certainty, that he had lost his soul. In the evening the patient's brother himself came over to us to ask our leader for medicine that might bring it back again.

8th of April. Samuel once more caught a big seal, and that was of course good, but he had also, unfortunately, punished his wife, my foster daughter Cecilie, who both cried and bled somewhat. It can not be denied that our womenfolk constantly give us cause for vexation, as they are poor examples of Christians for the heathens.

We were visited by a man from Sermilik, whom we initially could not recognize. It was

Marnêrak. He had, among other things, several deaths to report from there: Qâkajik's *(The Badly Worn Bench)* other wife Akumarpâjik had suddenly died, without disease, and the widow Suitsek *(Owner of Nothing)*, who had pains in her hips, had thrown herself into the sea.[41]

I had just come home from a visit to our "neighbors," where it was said that Sanimuinâq was now recovering well. (He slept when I was there). But immediately afterwards a message came which said that he was dying. Our leader and some of our people immediately went there. They thought, considering his speech, that he must have lost his mind. We since heard from others that he regarded himself as an *Ilisîtsok* (Soul taker).[42]

On the 13th of April, Maratssuk came and said that his younger brother was ill from a swelling in the neck, and that his mother–(the one who had frostbitten legs, and whom he had previously brought home in a sled)–was still ill,

41. Suicides were in certain circumstances viewed more with esteem than the opposite. In Christianised Greenland they were feared, however, and since they rarely or never occur openly here–they almost combine with the idea of "Fell-walking" or "qivineq."
42. It is striking that the scruples of the consciences of Angákuts, as well as those of normal people, which tend to emerge during fever fantasies–are always more or less about self-accusation, with them believing themselves to have become "Soul stealers."

and had soon decided to throw herself into the sea.

When my finger was bandaged this morning, a splinter of bone, which had broken out, was grabbed with some pliers and cut off with a pair of scissors.

Akorninaq *(One in Between)* is one of the only inhabited sites on the Angmagssalik Fjord where mussels can be found. A full bag was brought to us. Many people came with the first *umiak* of the year, but it was almost impossible to have a word with any one of them, as they ran around without rest, desiring only to see and feel all our things and possessions. At Akorninaq someone had caught a narwhal whose tusk was as long as a kayak paddle.

22nd of April. Today we took our *umiak* down from the scaffold so that I could start inspecting it for the return journey.

Sanimuínâk finally recovered from his illness, and has today caught a Hooded seal, and even did it by himself. But the carcass has been hidden away from him under the snow, as it is said that one should not bring a Hooded seal into the winter house. If you live in a tent, then it is another matter, then you are allowed to. It can only be called admirable that these people, as hungry as they might be, might, purely due to their great superstition, resist such a temptation as this: to eat the one thing that might strengthen their exhausted bodies, which they have come to possess!

Nápardlukoq *(Weakling)* had been luckier in this case, as he had only caught a Fjord seal–such a seal could be consumed immediately. The Fjord seal is otherwise a much less valuable seal when it comes to the quantity of meat provided compared to *ugssuk* or the Bearded seal.

On the 24th I worked a bit outside on our *umiak*, in spite of the fact that our leader wasn't really in favor of it, because of my finger.

On the 25th, ten foreign kayaks arrived to take part in the meal of Sanimuinâq's Hooded seal, which they now probably dared to eat. Some of them reported that the Kangârssuks had now moved out of their wintering site in three *umiaks*–some to Ikerasarssuaq and others to Qeqertarssuaq.

Today we put the skins for our new *umiak* cladding on to soak. Quaraq and Maqe *(material)* came walking overland from Sermilik.

⸸

1st of May. It rained this morning, but the weather became nice as the day progressed, with 8 degrees of warmth. It was Great Prayer Day, and we had four foreign Greenlanders take part in our service, and later in the day a whole lot of others too, including Kisime *(Alone)* and Qiaínaq–the latter the son of Qaratsserfik *(Lower Part of The Back of The Head).*

We had now torn down the outer part of our entrance passage to use the timber as fuel.

⸸

On the 2nd of May we were visited by Anginûq *(The Extremely Large Man),* Avâq, Upernâq *(Spring)* and Tamnejûq from Qeqertatssiaq.

Today we had torn some of the panelling down in our living room in order to obtain planks for *umiak* seats, and it was the first time I dared to participate properly since my finger had gone bad.

Our Europeans had heard of Ukutssiaq, who had become a widower, and had for three months now (according to custom) not been allowed to lie down on the bench (so he could only sleep in a seated position), and had for a similarly long time not been allowed to pull his hat down over his ears.

⚴

6th of May. Our Europeans returned today from an expedition to the warm spring, for which they had used the *umiaq* of Ukutssiaq. They were quite soaked, having fallen through the ice when they had had to get out of the boat. The warmth of the spring had been quite insignificant, they said–only ½ a degree.

The Easterlings helped us strap the skins on our *umiak*.

When a wife loses her husband, she herself dresses him in his kayak fur and puts his gloves on his hands, just like when he previously would go out in the kayak and needed to protect himself against frost and waves. She then jabs a stick in the arm bands, which she ties up very tightly. The stick is so the binding doesn't untie itself, and then she settles him down in the sea along with his kayak and additional accessories, or if the sea is frozen, at a hole in the ice.

Aluskât, who recently moved here, said to me today that since I didn't have my wife here to cook for me, I should just come and eat with them as often as I knew they had something to cook. But on this evening I was invited in to "our

Europeans."

Today we saw a flock of geese flying in over the land.

⁂

11th of May. When Aluskât wanted to journey out to collect *quperdlûssat* (a different edible root than the aforementioned *tugdlerungnaq*) I came along in order to see the processing of a seal stashed by Samuel on the way, but I was not entirely unafraid in such an incredibly small *umiak* as those of these people.

Upon our return I gladly learned that Johan had shot his first Fjord seal. Offshore wind today, with clear and quiet weather.

⁂

On the 13th Debora and Severine went with Qutsuluk's *umiak* into the Fjord to collect mussels while we were visited by the *umiak* of Amatsineq. The kayakers, during this time of a new moon, travelled from site to site visiting each other according to their strange custom of wife-swapping.

⁂

The 20th. The day before yesterday I covered

the nails on our *umiak* and greased them with blubber, and similarly fashioned oars. Yesterday I sewed tent strings and guy ropes for the tent, caulked the nails a second time and did various other small things in preparation for our departure and later caught a little bird, the tail of which was longer than its body. It was smaller than a regular finch and our Europeans said that it really belonged in Egypt.

✝

On the 29th, in the morning the fog had lifted and there was a bit of an offshore wind, but the ice has long lain closely packed against the land.

Uggunárqusimassoq[43] was here today. He still grieved over his son perishing in his kayak over the winter. He had come to divert his sorrow through external things, he said, for which reason I showed him everything I could think of. But then at the end I said, "Now you have seen the things which I had at my disposal, and delighted over what I have told you, but you will not gain any durable comfort from your sorrow–for all this will soon disappear from you again. Am I not right?" He said, "Yes," after which I spoke to him of the comfort of sorrowful Christians, and about

43. *Uggunârqusimassoq is a leader who says: "Here–this way!"*

how he would, after death, once more see the son he grieved so deeply for. I also showed him biblical pictures, which I explained as best I could. He did also seem thankful, but was vexed, he said, by the fact that he would probably forget it all later.

30th of May. Today I made some preparations for the set-up of the cairn that our leader also wanted to erect here as a commemoration of our stay, and in the event that we didn't make it back ourselves, that others might some time learn that we had made it to the farthest destination of our journey.

Trinity Sunday, 31st of May. I did not get to hold a service, as there was too much unrest in all of us, partially over building the cairn here, but particularly also in getting the boats sorted in order to make a little visit at the herring site at the base of the fjord, where 225 people in tents now stand in one place. It had originally been *Sáakutôq's* intent to leave here for good the moment we finished our preparations, but right now the drift ice lies quite unusually closely packed in towards us. We built our cairn eight feet high, whereafter we all, with the exception of Cecilie, who was suffering an abscess, were posed around it and photographed.

We wrote the 1st of June the day we travelled by boat to the herring site. On the way we met 25 kayaks, who showed great pleasure in seeing us. There stood twenty tents with 12 *umiaks* altogether, but the herring which they had travelled there for had only been encountered in poor quantities. We constantly went round visiting and got enough herring for ourselves. There was also a bit of fun of the winterly type, with dancing, ballads and snow games, and one of the women, old Palasêq, danced a fool-dance with a drum. In the evening I held a service and spoke a lot with them about religious matters, and when I finally told them "goodbye," they again expressed the wish to have Christian teachers sent to them, and several of them were moved when I mentioned that we would now be unlikely to see each other ever again.

9th of June. On the night of the 8th I slept in a tent for the first time since winter, and we were now really busy with the finalities! Samuel even got two Fjord seals.

⁂

21st of June. And then we finally left our wintering site Tassiussârssuk! The weather was cloudy and warm, with some gusts of *nigek*. Just as we were to set off, Uggunârqussimassoq came to pick up the trifles which we had left behind. On our way out we encountered Kisimé in a kayak. He had also caught two Fjord seals. We took them into the boat, whereupon he turned around and followed us a bit of the way, then he and Samuel soon caught a Bearded seal.

It was quiet, with slightly overcast skies. And that day we finally lost sight of the fells of our Angmagsalik!

Afterword
by Signe Rink

In order not to extend the present extract beyond the main intent, we will depart from the wording of Hansen's well kept diary to now complete the journey in a couple of very long leaps, inasmuch that the expedition's return journey roughly followed the same route as the journey up, and was marked by quite similar events, only in the reverse order; they met with the same heathen companies of the east coast's more southern group, mostly stopped at the same sites, travelled on the same ice and once more met, among others, the expedition's native depot custodian, the "magnificent Navfalik", as I repeatedly recall him mentioned in Commander Holm's own work on this expedition.

On the 16th of July they had the pleasure of encountering the rescue section led by the then Lieutenant Garde. From the latter they learned how the winter had elapsed in West Greenland, of which Hansen in particular could be pleased, through the report that his wife had given him a daughter.

They then once more passed the Puissortoq glacier with Karrit-Akornat; later Aluk, Pamiagdluk, Nanortalik and Agdluitsup-pâ (Hansen's own home), until they could finally enter the main colony Julianehaab safe and sound. The stay was not a long one, as they immediately learned that the trade ship "Constance" was awaiting them in the outer harbor, Qagssimiut.

Hansêrak ends his diary with the following words:

You encounter fears and dangers everywhere;
but God's care is the same anywhere.
Thanks be to Him!